THE Woodsmith COLLECTION™

CLASSIC CABINETS

From the Editors and Staff of
Woodsmith® Magazine

AUGUST HOME PUBLISHING COMPANY
DES MOINES, IOWA

AUGUST HOME
PUBLISHING COMPANY

Publisher   Donald B. Peschke

August Home Books

Executive Editor   Douglas L. Hicks
Art Director   Linda F. Vermie
Senior Graphic Designer   Chris Glowacki
Graphic Design Intern   Vu Nguyen
Copy Editor   David Stone
Contributing Book Designer   Ted Kralicek

Contributing Staff

Editor, *Woodsmith*   Terry J. Strohman
Art Director, *Woodsmith*   Todd Lambirth
Editor, *ShopNotes*   Tim Robertson
Art Director, *ShopNotes*   Cary Christensen
Editor, *Workbench*   Chris Inman
Art Director, *Workbench*   Robert Foss

Creative Director   Ted Kralicek
Project Design Developer   Ken Munkel
Project Designers   Kent Welsh
Ted Wong
Project Builders   Steve Curtis
Steve Johnson
Editors   Vincent S. Ancona
Jon Garbison
Bryan Nelson
Phil Totten
Illustrators   Mark Higdon
David Kreyling
Erich Lage
Mike Mittermeier
Roger Reiland
Kurt Schultz
Cinda Shambaugh
Dirk Ver Steeg
Photographers   Lark Smothermon
Crayola England
Production Director   George Chmielarz
Production   Douglas M. Lidster
Troy A. Clark
V.P. Planning & Finance   Jon Macarthy
Sales & Marketing   Bob Baker
Kent A. Buckton
New Media Manager   Gordon C. Gaippe

If you have any questions or comments about this book or would like subscription information about *Woodsmith*, *ShopNotes*, or *Workbench* magazines, please write to:

August Home Publishing Co.
2200 Grand Ave.
Des Moines, IA 50312

Or call: 1 800–444–7527
Internet: http://www.augusthome.com

INTRODUCTION

What's a "classic" cabinet? Does that mean it's big — and complicated? Well, it's true that most of the projects in this book are big. But they're not really that complicated.

Okay, I know there are lots of parts, joints, and procedures in most of these cabinets and that all may seem a little intimidating. But that's only if you look at the project as a "whole." What I like to do is break a big project down into a series of "mini-projects."

Take the Display Cabinet on pages 66 to 73 for example. First you make the lower case. It's simply a plywood box with some facings and moldings applied. You might be able to get it done in a day.

Then you're on to the next mini-project: the upper case. After that, it's the back frame, the top molding, the doors, and the shelves. Sure it's going to take you a number of weekends to finish all of these mini-projects. But I find a certain satisfaction in completing at least one part of a project every time I go into my shop.

Once all of the parts are done, you put them together and get a Display Cabinet.

So that's how we decided to present the projects in this book. Each one is broken down into units that are manageable and can be completed in a relatively short period of time.

I hope this is helpful as you build some of these Classic Cabinets.

Doug

NOTE: This is a special "Heavy-Duty Shop Edition" of *Classic Cabinets*. We've printed it with the following features to make it easier to use in your shop:
• UNIQUE "LAY-FLAT" BINDING — Don't be afraid to press down hard at the center between the pages. Open it anywhere and try it. It will stay flat and won't flap shut. You can't "crack" the binding.
• COLD RESISTANT — The special cold-set glue used in the binding stays strong and flexible. Even in a below-freezing garage shop.
• LAMINATED COVER — Resists dirt, liquids, stains, and many finishes.
• LOW-GLARE, HEAVY-DUTY PAPER — It's easy-to-read, even under bright shop lights.

CONTENTS

Page 15

Page 23

Page 78

APOTHECARY CABINET

To build this cherry box full of boxes, there's just a few basic machine setups to do — and then lots of repeat cuts.

There's a certain fascination with drawers. For many people it's "What can they hold?" In the case of this apothecary cabinet, just about anything smaller than a shoe.

But the drawers might raise a different question from a woodworker. Such as "How do they work?" Or, "How are they built?" The answer to both of these questions is the same — very simply. The drawers fit in the cabinet with no special hardware. And they're built in a low-tech way, too.

JOINERY. The joinery used on the drawers is the same joinery that holds the entire cabinet together, rabbets and dadoes. They're a couple of the most versatile joints in woodworking.

There's one thing about dadoes and rabbets — they must be cut perfectly. That's because when the cabinet is assembled there are no screws or nails to reinforce the joints, just glue. Plus, the joints will be visible.

FINISH. Ordinarily when I build a project using cherry, I leave the wood

unstained. But this project was different, and the reason was the knobs. The knobs I thought looked best for the drawers weren't available in cherry, only birch. And if you've ever tried to stain a light wood (such as birch) to match a darker wood (cherry), you know what a challenge it can be.

Instead of trying to match the natural color of the drawer fronts, I stained the knobs a darker color. Then, for contrast, I stained the rest of the cabinet the same color as the knobs.

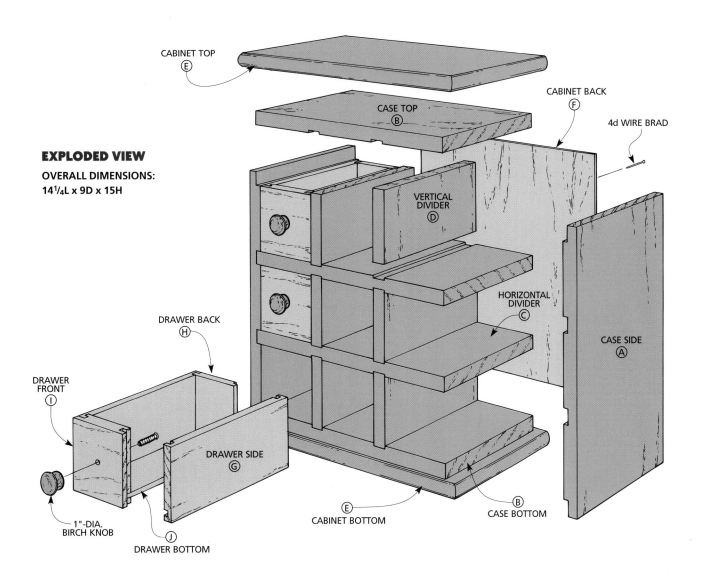

EXPLODED VIEW
OVERALL DIMENSIONS:
14¼L x 9D x 15H

MATERIALS LIST

A Case Sides (2)   ¾ x 8⅝ - 13½
B Case Top/Bottom (2)   ¾ x 8⅜ - 12½
C Horiz. Dividers (2)   ¾ x 8⅜ - 12½
D Vertical Dividers (6)   ¾ x 8⅜ - 3¾
E Cabinet Top/Bott. (2)   ¾ x 9 - 14¼
F Cabinet Back (1)   ¼ ply - 12½ x 13½
G Drawer Sides (18)   ½ x 3⁷⁄₁₆ - 8⅛
H Drawer Backs (9)   ½ x 3⁷⁄₁₆ - 2¹⁵⁄₁₆
I Drawer Fronts (9)   ¾ x 3⁷⁄₁₆ - 3⁷⁄₁₆
J Drawer Bottoms (9)   ¼ ply - 2⅞ x 7⁹⁄₁₆

HARDWARE SUPPLIES
(9) 1"-dia. birch knobs with screws

CUTTING DIAGRAM

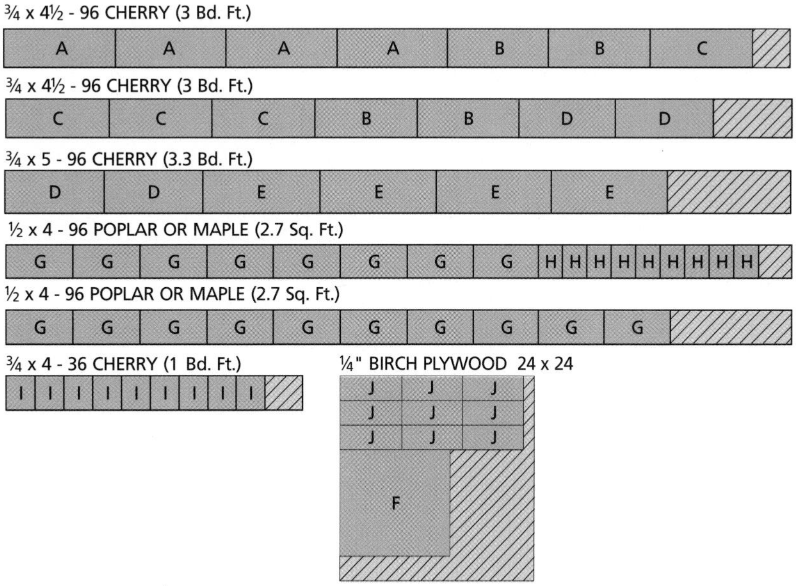

¾ x 4½ - 96 CHERRY (3 Bd. Ft.)

| A | A | A | A | B | B | C | |

¾ x 4½ - 96 CHERRY (3 Bd. Ft.)

| C | C | C | B | B | D | D | |

¾ x 5 - 96 CHERRY (3.3 Bd. Ft.)

| D | D | E | E | E | E | |

½ x 4 - 96 POPLAR OR MAPLE (2.7 Sq. Ft.)

| G | G | G | G | G | G | G | G | H H H H H H H H |

½ x 4 - 96 POPLAR OR MAPLE (2.7 Sq. Ft.)

| G | G | G | G | G | G | G | G | G | |

¾ x 4 - 36 CHERRY (1 Bd. Ft.)

| I | I | I | I | I | I | I | I | I | |

¼" BIRCH PLYWOOD 24 x 24

J	J	J
J	J	J
J	J	J

F

PREPARING THE PANELS

I cut the parts for most projects only when I'm ready for them. But sometimes there's a good reason to cut the parts in advance. On this project, the reason is the joinery. The parts fit together with dadoes and rabbets; see Fig. 3 below. This means they must start out the same thickness, then the joints can all be cut the same.

I started by edge-gluing an *oversize* blank for each part; see drawings below. (Note: Glue up the blanks *larger* than the finished dimensions shown.)

THICKNESS. Before cutting the blanks to finished size, they should all be planed to the same thickness ($3/4$"). And to ensure good-fitting joinery, it helps to check the thickness of each part in a test dado. I cut this dado using a $3/4$" straight bit in the router.

DADOES & RABBETS

After the panels have all been planed to the same thickness, the individual parts (A, B, and C) can be cut to finished length and width; see drawings at left.

Note: Set aside the oversized blank for the vertical dividers (D) and the top/bottom blanks (E) for now. They'll be cut to finished size later.

DADOES & RABBETS. When the case parts have been cut to size, the dadoes and rabbets can be cut.

Note: Because these cuts will be visible on the front of the cabinet, you want the bottoms to be perfectly flat and the sides square. So I used a $3/4$" straight bit in the router table; see Figs. 1 and 2. A stack dado set will also work, but only the very best will cut as accurately as a straight bit.

All the dadoes and rabbets can be cut with the same bit. But a number of different router table setups are needed.

CASE SIDES. First, I routed the rabbets on the top and bottom of the sides (A); see Fig. 3a.

Next, I routed the dadoes across the sides; see Fig. 3b. These are critical cuts. With the fence adjusted to the proper distance from the router bit ($4^{1}/4$"), the dadoes on each workpiece will create equal-size openings when the cabinet is assembled.

The third setup is for cutting a rabbet to accept the plywood back. For this, the router table fence must be repositioned to rout a $1/4$" x $1/4$" rabbet on the back edges of the side pieces (A).

TOP & BOTTOM. Now the case sides can be set aside for a moment. Then, lower the router bit to cut the remaining dadoes on the case top/bottom (one side only) and horizontal dividers (both sides); see Fig. 3c.

Next, I moved on to the dividers.

VERTICAL DIVIDERS

After the dadoes and rabbets have been cut on the case parts, the pieces can be dry assembled to test the fit. Note: The parts should be assembled so they're all flush across the front of the assembly. And the back edges of the horizontal pieces (the top/bottom and horizontal dividers) should align to the inside edge of the rabbets cut for the plywood back; refer to Fig. 7.

VERTICAL DIVIDERS. Now, work can begin on the vertical dividers. The first

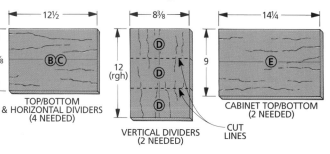

SIDES
(2 NEEDED)

$8^{5}/8$ $13^{1}/2$

TOP/BOTTOM
& HORIZONTAL DIVIDERS
(4 NEEDED)

$12^{1}/2$ $8^{3}/8$ B C

VERTICAL DIVIDERS
(2 NEEDED)

$8^{3}/8$ 12 (rgh) D D D CUT LINES

CABINET TOP/BOTTOM
(2 NEEDED)

$14^{1}/4$ 9 E

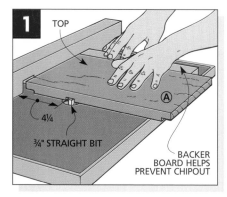

1 TOP

$4^{1}/4$

$3/4$" STRAIGHT BIT

A A

BACKER
BOARD HELPS
PREVENT CHIPOUT

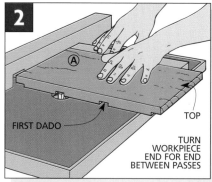

2 A

FIRST DADO

TOP

TURN
WORKPIECE
END FOR END
BETWEEN PASSES

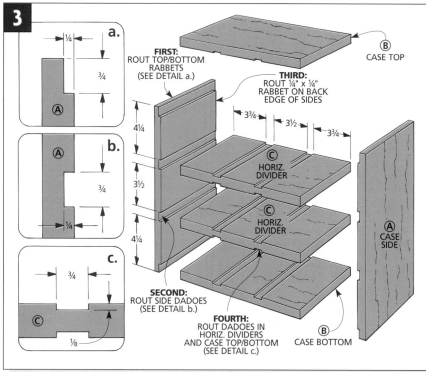

3

a. $1/4$ $3/4$ A

b. A $3/4$ $1/4$

c. $3/4$ C $1/8$

FIRST:
ROUT TOP/BOTTOM
RABBETS
(SEE DETAIL a.)

THIRD:
ROUT $1/4$" x $1/4$"
RABBET ON BACK
EDGE OF SIDES

CASE TOP B

$4^{1}/4$ $3^{3}/4$ $3^{1}/2$ $3^{3}/4$

C HORIZ.
DIVIDER

$3^{1}/2$

C HORIZ.
DIVIDER

$4^{1}/4$

A
CASE
SIDE

SECOND:
ROUT SIDE DADOES
(SEE DETAIL b.)

FOURTH:
ROUT DADOES IN
HORIZ. DIVIDERS
AND CASE TOP/BOTTOM
(SEE DETAIL c.)

CASE BOTTOM B

thing to do is rip the blank for the dividers to finished width (the same width as the horizontal dividers, 8³/₈"), refer to the drawings at the top of page 6.

Now the dividers (D) can be cut to finished length (height). But instead of cutting each piece in one pass using the miter gauge on the table saw, I did something different. (Again, the reasoning was to cut all the dividers exactly the same length.)

First, dry assemble and measure between the bottoms of each pair of dadoes; see Fig. 4. Then cut each blank into three oversize pieces (slightly longer than the dado-to-dado height); see Fig. 5. Note that the grain runs vertically on the dividers; refer to Fig. 4.

Now the dividers can be cut to finished length by trimming the slightly-long blanks one at a time using the table saw in conjunction with the rip fence; see Fig. 6.

Safety Note: I don't ordinarily cut a workpiece to length using the rip fence. But since the widest edge of the piece is against the fence, the procedure is as safe as an ordinary rip cut. Even though the piece is being cut to finished length.

FINAL ASSEMBLY

When the vertical dividers have all been fitted inside the case, I added a top and bottom then a plywood back.

ASSEMBLY. First, I disassembled the case then put it back together again with glue in all the joints. It's easiest to start from the outside and work toward the center.

TOP & BOTTOM. Next, cut a cabinet top and bottom (E) to fit on the case. Note: Cut these pieces to create a ³/₈" overhang on the front and sides; see Fig. 7b. (They will be installed flush at the back of the case.)

Then, before attaching the top and bottom, I routed a bullnose profile on the sides and front (not the back); see Fig. 7a.

Finally, I glued the top and bottom onto the case. A couple nipped-off brads keep the panels from slipping around when they're glued and clamped in place; see Fig. 7b.

BACK. Finally, cut a piece of ¹/₄" plywood for the cabinet back (F). Note: The back fits in the rabbets in the case sides, and between the top and bottom pieces (E); see Fig. 7. Short brads secure it to the case.

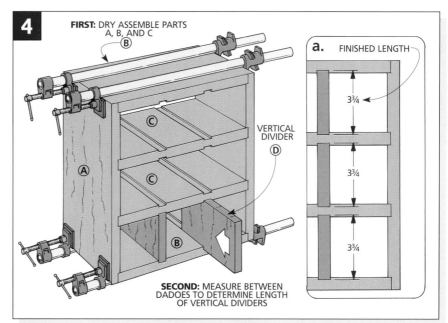

4

FIRST: DRY ASSEMBLE PARTS A, B, AND C

VERTICAL DIVIDER D

SECOND: MEASURE BETWEEN DADOES TO DETERMINE LENGTH OF VERTICAL DIVIDERS

a. FINISHED LENGTH

3³/₄

3³/₄

3³/₄

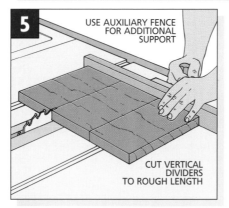

5 USE AUXILIARY FENCE FOR ADDITIONAL SUPPORT

CUT VERTICAL DIVIDERS TO ROUGH LENGTH

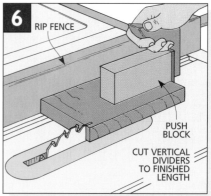

6 RIP FENCE

PUSH BLOCK

CUT VERTICAL DIVIDERS TO FINISHED LENGTH

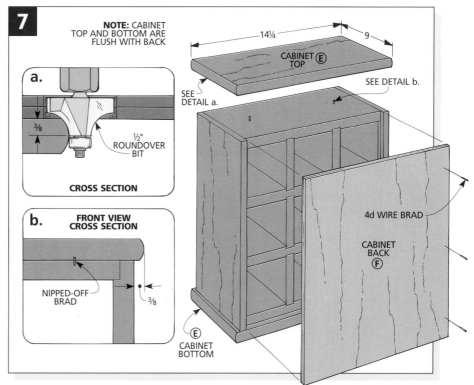

7 **NOTE:** CABINET TOP AND BOTTOM ARE FLUSH WITH BACK

14¹/₄   9

CABINET TOP E

SEE DETAIL a.

SEE DETAIL b.

a.

³/₈

¹/₂" ROUNDOVER BIT

CROSS SECTION

b. **FRONT VIEW CROSS SECTION**

NIPPED-OFF BRAD

³/₈

4d WIRE BRAD

CABINET BACK F

E CABINET BOTTOM

DRAWERS

What makes this cabinet useful are the drawers. And they're all made the same way in a series of repetitive cuts. Locking rabbet joints hold the parts together; refer to Figs. 8a and b.

CUT TO SIZE. The key to making multiple drawers is the setup. If the drawer openings are all the same size ($3\frac{1}{2}$" square), the parts for the drawers can all be cut to uniform sizes.

Note: The drawer sides (G) and backs (H) are cut from $\frac{1}{2}$"-thick stock, and the fronts (I) are cut from $\frac{3}{4}$"-thick stock.

When the parts have been cut, work can begin on the locking rabbets joints.

DRAWER JOINTS. There are just a few steps required to make the joints for the drawers. And the cuts can be made with three different setups using a $\frac{1}{4}$" straight bit in the router table.

Shop Note: To prevent the small workpieces from tipping into the large bit opening in my router table, I closed up the opening by adding a "zero-clearance" overlay on top of my table. It's a piece of $\frac{1}{4}$" hardboard with a small bit opening; see Fig. 9. I held it to the top of my router table with carpet tape.

Also, for tight-fitting joints, it helps to start with test cuts on scrap wood.

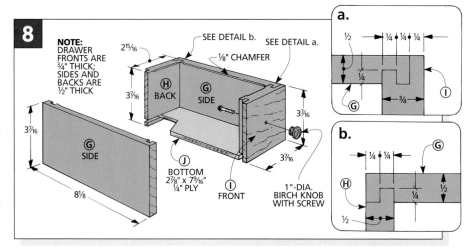

DADOES AND GROOVES. The first cut to make is a $\frac{1}{4}$" dado near the front and back of each drawer side (G); see Fig. 9. Position the fence so the distance from the *outside* of the bit to the fence equals the thickness of the drawer back ($\frac{1}{2}$"); see Fig. 9a.

Now, with the same setup, rout a groove on all the drawer parts for the drawer bottom; see Fig. 10. For the groove on the drawer sides, plunge the piece onto the bit and rout from the front dado to the back dado; see Fig. 10a.

TONGUES. Next, tongues are routed on the drawer front and back to fit the grooves in the sides. First, raise the

height of the bit, but don't move the fence; see Fig. 11a. Then hold the drawer front on edge and run it over the bit; see Fig. 11.

To complete the tongues, lower the bit ($\frac{1}{4}$" high) and reposition the fence; see Fig. 12a. Then run the drawer fronts and backs over the bit; see Fig. 12.

ASSEMBLY. Now the $\frac{1}{4}$" plywood drawer bottoms (J) can be cut to fit between the grooves; see Fig. 8. And, finally, the drawer parts glued together.

CHAMFER. Once the glue dried, I softened the top *inside* edge of each drawer by using the router table to rout a narrow ($\frac{1}{8}$") chamfer. ■

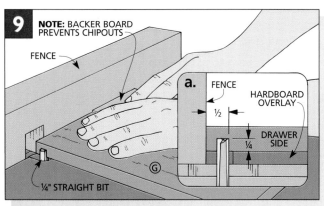

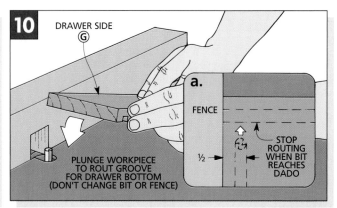

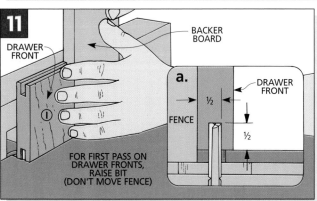

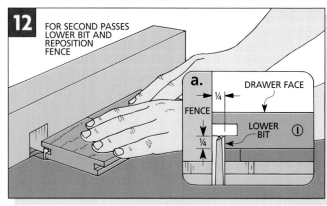

COLLECTOR'S CABINET

This cabinet is built with two different miter joints — end miters and face miters. Then splines are added to strengthen the joints.

Almost everyone I know has a collection of something — small toys, figurines, or items that simply bring back fond memories. This cabinet is a perfect place to hold and protect them.

It's made of three components: the case, the dividers, and the doors.

THE CASE. There's nothing complicated about building the case — it's simply a shallow box with mitered corners. To help align these corners and make them stronger, I cut kerfs in the ends and joined them together with hardwood splines.

To mount the case to the wall, I used a hidden interlocking hanging system.

It's a two–part system that holds the case securely to the wall.

THE DIVIDERS. The second part of the cabinet, the dividers, is the most challenging. The problem is collections change over time, and require different divider locations.

To solve the problem, the dividers are not glued in place, but are held by a "friction fit" in shallow dadoes. This allows the pieces to be removed and then dadoed if you wish to add more dividers. Or insert new pieces without dadoes if you want fewer dividers.

THE DOORS. The third part of this cabinet is the doors. Here again I used splines to align and strengthen the mitered corners. However, the technique for cutting the kerfs to accept the splines is slightly different. It's featured in a technique section on page 14.

MATERIALS. To keep the items in the cabinet from getting lost in the shadows, I wanted a light background. So I built the cabinet and all of the dividers out of hard maple. Then I used 1/4" maple plywood for the back panel.

FINISH. To finish the cabinet and dividers I wiped on two coats of General Finishes' Royal Finish, a tung oil and urethane combination.

EXPLODED VIEW … COLLECTOR'S CABINET

OVERALL DIMENSIONS:
25¼W x 18¼H x 4D

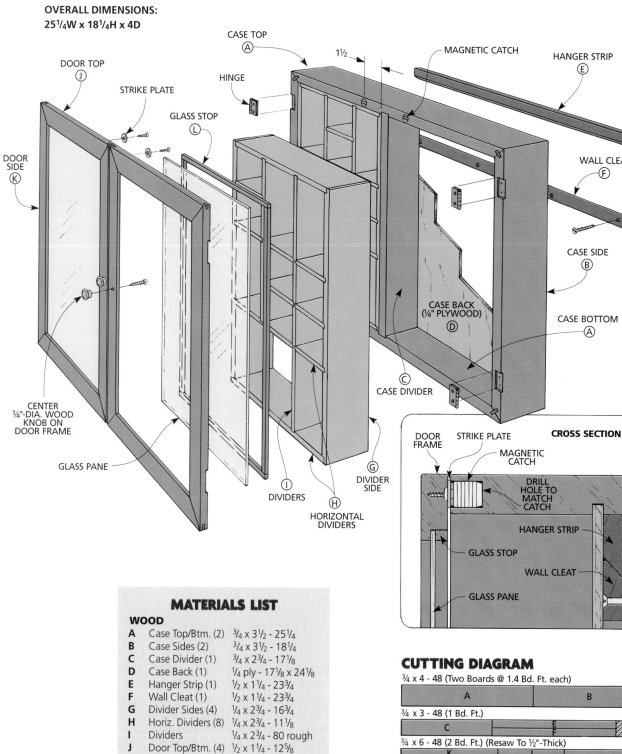

CASE TOP
Ⓐ

HINGE

1½

MAGNETIC CATCH

HANGER STRIP
Ⓔ

DOOR TOP
Ⓙ

STRIKE PLATE

GLASS STOP
Ⓛ

DOOR SIDE
Ⓚ

WALL CLEAT
Ⓕ

CASE SIDE
Ⓑ

CASE BACK
(¼" PLYWOOD)
Ⓓ

CASE BOTTOM
Ⓐ

CENTER
¾"-DIA. WOOD
KNOB ON
DOOR FRAME

GLASS PANE

CASE DIVIDER
Ⓒ

DIVIDERS
Ⓘ

HORIZONTAL
DIVIDERS
Ⓗ

DIVIDER SIDE
Ⓖ

CROSS SECTION

DOOR FRAME   STRIKE PLATE

MAGNETIC CATCH

DRILL HOLE TO MATCH CATCH

HANGER STRIP

GLASS STOP

WALL CLEAT

GLASS PANE

MATERIALS LIST

WOOD

A	Case Top/Btm. (2)	¾ x 3½ - 25¼
B	Case Sides (2)	¾ x 3½ - 18¼
C	Case Divider (1)	¾ x 2¾ - 17⅛
D	Case Back (1)	¼ ply - 17⅛ x 24⅛
E	Hanger Strip (1)	½ x 1¼ - 23¾
F	Wall Cleat (1)	½ x 1¼ - 23¾
G	Divider Sides (4)	¼ x 2¾ - 16¾
H	Horiz. Dividers (8)	¼ x 2¾ - 11⅛
I	Dividers	¼ x 2¾ - 80 rough
J	Door Top/Btm. (4)	½ x 1¼ - 12⅝
K	Door Sides (4)	½ x 1¼ - 18¼
L	Glass Stops (8)	3/16 x 5/16 - 16¼ rough

HARDWARE SUPPLIES

(4) 1 1/16"-wide x 1¼"-long Butt hinges
(2) ¾"-dia. Wooden knobs
(2) Magnetic catches with strike plates
(2) 1/8"-thick Glass, cut to fit

CUTTING DIAGRAM

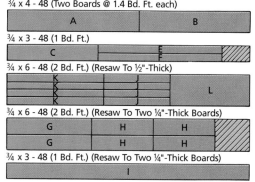

¾ x 4 - 48 (Two Boards @ 1.4 Bd. Ft. each)

A	B

¾ x 3 - 48 (1 Bd. Ft.)

C	E

¾ x 6 - 48 (2 Bd. Ft.) (Resaw To ½"-Thick)

K	L
K	
K	

¾ x 6 - 48 (2 Bd. Ft.) (Resaw To Two ¼"-Thick Boards)

G	H	H
G	H	H

¾ x 3 - 48 (1 Bd. Ft.) (Resaw To Two ¼"-Thick Boards)

I

NOTE: ALSO NEED 2' x 4' SHEET OF ¼" PLYWOOD.

CASE

The dimensions of this cabinet are based on the divider layout shown in Fig. 4 on page 12. In fact, to make this project fit this divider layout, you want to make sure the *inside* dimensions of each half of the finished case are exactly $11\frac{1}{2}$" wide by $16\frac{3}{4}$" high. If you change these dimensions, you will have to change the divider layout also.

TOP, BOTTOM, AND SIDES. I started by cutting the top/bottom (A) from $\frac{3}{4}$" stock to a rough length of 27". Then cut the sides (B) to a rough length of 20". Now rip all four pieces to a width of $3\frac{1}{2}$"; see Fig. 1.

Next, the ends of these pieces are mitered to length and joined together with hardwood splines. To miter the pieces to length, tilt your saw blade to 45° and miter one end off all four pieces. Then miter the other end of the top and bottom pieces (A) to a finished length of $25\frac{1}{4}$" (long point to long point). And miter the sides (B) to a finished length of $18\frac{1}{4}$"; see Fig. 1.

SPLINED MITER. Once the pieces are cut to length, I cut kerfs in the mitered ends to hold splines; see Fig. 1a. Then I cut splines from scrap hardwood to fit the kerfs.

GROOVE FOR THE BACK. Next a groove is cut in the top, bottom, and side pieces for the plywood back. The front edge of this groove is located $\frac{3}{4}$" in from the back edge of all four pieces; see Fig. 2a. The extra space at the back will be needed to conceal the special hanging system that is used to hold the cabinet on the wall; refer to Fig. 3.

DIVIDER. The next step is to cut dadoes to hold the $\frac{3}{4}$"-thick case divider (C); see Fig. 1b. These dadoes are centered on the length of the top/bottom pieces (A) and are cut to the same width as the thickness of the divider ($\frac{3}{4}$").

With the dadoes completed, the divider (C) can be cut to a finished width of $2\frac{3}{4}$". To determine the length of the divider, dry-assemble the case and cut the divider to fit between the dadoes.

ASSEMBLY. After the grooves and dadoes are cut in the pieces, I cut a piece of $\frac{1}{4}$" plywood to use as the case back (D). Then glue and clamp the case with band clamps; see Fig. 2.

Shop Note: To provide even clamping pressure and protect the corners of the case, I made small clamping blocks from pieces of 2x2 stock.

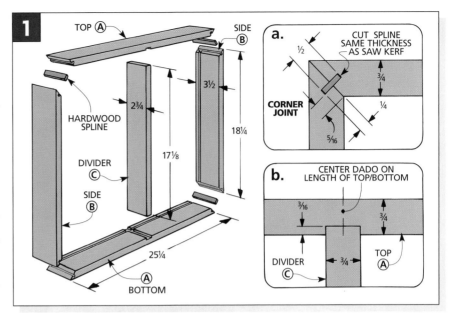

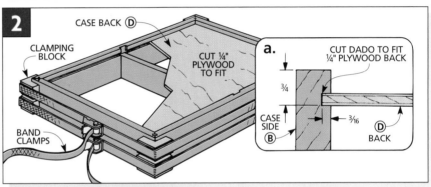

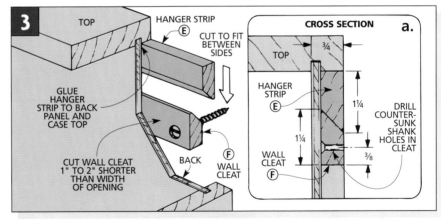

HANGING SYSTEM

It's difficult to hang a cabinet like this level and secure. To make things easier, I like to use an invisible hanging system built right into the design of the cabinet.

INTERLOCKING STRIPS. The system consists of two interlocking strips that are concealed behind the cabinet; see Fig. 3. The hanger strip (E) is glued to the back of the cabinet and the wall cleat (F) is screwed to the wall studs.

CUT THE PIECES. To make the $\frac{1}{2}$"-thick strips, tilt the saw blade to 45°. Then bevel-rip two 24"-long pieces, $1\frac{1}{4}$" wide; see Fig. 3a. Trim one strip (E) to fit between the sides in the back of the cabinet and glue it in place.

To allow for some side-to-side adjustment, I cut the remaining strip (F) 1" or 2" shorter than the one glued to the cabinet. This cleat will be screwed to the wall stud and the cabinet set over it so the pieces interlock; see Fig. 3a.

DIVIDER UNITS

The next thing to make is the divider units — one for each side of the case. The dividers are removable so they can be changed as your collection changes.

THICKNESS STOCK. The key to making the dividers removable is to cut the pieces to thickness so they fit a $1/4$"-wide dado. The dividers should fit snugly, but not overly tight. To get the correct fit, I cut a $1/4$" dado in a test piece. Then I resawed and planed $2^3/4$"-wide stock until it fit the test dado.

SIDE PIECES. To make the two divider units, cut four sides (G) to fit the height of the case openings; see Fig. 5. Then cut a $1/16$"-deep rabbet on the ends of these pieces; see Fig. 5a.

HORIZONTAL DIVIDERS. Now you have to decide where you want the dividers. I used the layouts in Fig. 4.

My layout starts out by positioning two $1/16$"-deep dadoes on the divider sides (G) to create three equally-spaced horizontal sections; see Fig. 5.

After these pieces are dadoed, place them in the case. Then cut the horizontal dividers (H) to fit between them.

Note: If you want to display large items, don't divide the case any farther; refer to the inset photo on page 9.

LAYOUT GAUGE. To help divide the case into smaller sections, I made a layout gauge from scrap wood; see Fig. 6.

The size of the gauge is determined by dividing the main horizontal sections into six equal-sized compartments ($2^1/2$" high by $3^1/2$" long); refer to Fig. 4.

MORE DIVIDERS. To locate the dadoes for the vertical dividers, place the gauge tight against one of the divider sides; see Fig. 6. Mark the dado locations on the top and bottom of that sec-

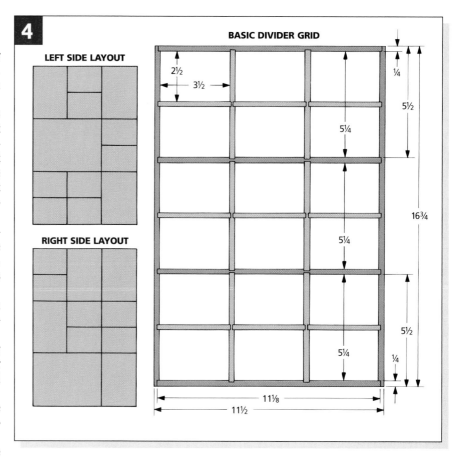

4

LEFT SIDE LAYOUT

RIGHT SIDE LAYOUT

BASIC DIVIDER GRID

tion and cut $1/16$"-deep dadoes at the marks. Then cut the vertical dividers to fit and push them in place.

Next, horizontal dividers can be installed. Here again I used the gauge to determine their locations; see Fig. 7.

DOORS

With the dividers complete, work can begin on the doors. These doors are assembled like picture frames.

CUTTING THE STOCK. To make the doors, start by resawing $1/2$"-thick stock

for the $1^1/4$"-wide top/bottom (J), and sides (K); see Fig. 8a. Then cut all of the pieces for both doors to rough length.

To form a lip for the glass to rest in, cut a $3/16$" x $3/8$" rabbet on the inside face of each of the pieces; see Fig. 8b.

MITER TO LENGTH. Next, the top, bottom, and side pieces are mitered to finished length; see Fig. 8. To determine the length of the tops/bottoms (J), measure the width of the case ($25^1/4$") and divide in half ($12^5/8$"). The sides (K) are the same length as the height of the case ($18^1/4$"); see Fig. 8.

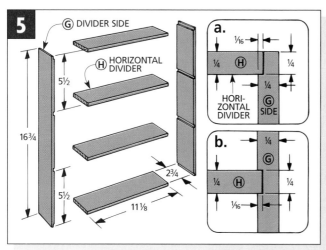

5

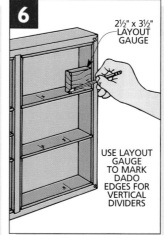

6

7

KERF THE ENDS. Now kerfs can be cut in the mitered ends for the splines; see Fig. 9. For more information on cutting the kerfs and splines see page 14.

ASSEMBLY. After the miters and splines are cut, the doors are ready to be assembled. To make sure the doors fit the case correctly, I used the case as a guide; see Fig. 10.

Start by clamping one of the side pieces (K) to the case. Align the side edge of the piece flush with the side of the case and position the rabbet down.

INSERT SPLINES. Next, put glue on two splines and push them into the kerfs. The splines are extra long and will be trimmed flush later; see Fig. 9a.

Now, glue the top and bottom pieces to the side piece. Then, insert the splines and glue and clamp the remaining side piece in place. To make the other door, repeat the procedure.

TRIM SPLINES. When the glue on the doors is dry, the splines can be trimmed flush; refer to Step 6 on page 14.

HINGE MORTISES. The next step is to attach the doors. To do this, I mortised four 1¼"-long brass butt hinges into the case and doors; see Fig. 11.

Start by scribing the mortises with a sharp knife, 2" in from the top and bottom of the case. Then transfer the mortise locations to the inside of the doors. Now rout or chisel out the mortises to the depth of the hinge leaf, and screw the hinges in place; see Fig. 11a.

INSTALL GLASS. To complete the doors you just have to install the glass and glue in the glass stops. To determine the size of the glass, measure the rabbeted opening of each door and subtract 1/16" to allow for easy clearance.

GLASS STOPS. Once the glass is cut, the glass stops (L) can be made. These stops are hardwood strips that are glued into the rabbets; see Fig. 12.

Shop Note: It's tricky to get the stops flush with the inside face of the doors. To solve this problem, I made the stops so they're slightly "proud" when they're installed; see Fig. 12. (In my case this means the stops are 5/16" thick.) Then I planed them down flush with a block plane.

One more thing about the stops. When you glue them in just put a small drop of glue every 2"; see Fig. 12. This way they'll be easier to remove if you ever have to replace the glass.

WOODEN KNOBS. To finish off the cabinet, I added a couple of wooden knobs to open the doors; refer to the Exploded View on page 10.

FINISHING. Now all of the dividers can be removed and finish applied to the whole project.

MAGNETIC CATCHES. The last step is to install magnetic catches to each door; refer to the Cross Section on page 10. To do this, drill two holes in the top edge of the case that match the size of the catches. Locate these holes 1½" on either side of the case divider. Then glue the magnetic catches in place. Finally, screw the strike plates to the inside of the doors. ■

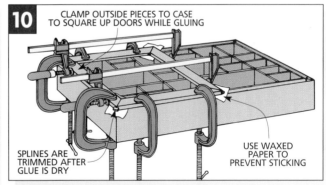

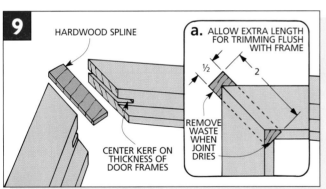

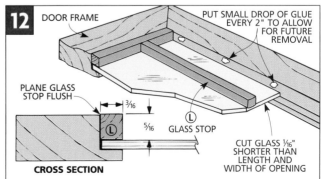

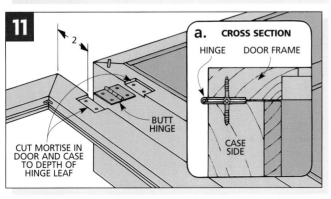

When making the doors for the collector's cabinet shown on page 9, I used a spline in the mitered corners to align and strengthen the joint. To do this, kerfs are cut in the mitered ends of the door pieces.

These kerfs are cut by running the mitered ends over the table saw blade. The problem is that it's difficult to hold the workpiece securely at an angle while making this cut. To solve the problem, I made a simple plywood jig to support the pieces while cutting the kerfs in the ends; see Step 3 below.

Once the kerfs are cut, thin hardwood splines can be made to fit the kerfs. The easiest way to do this is to

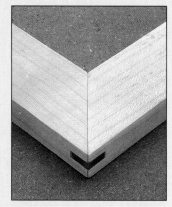

cut the splines off the edge of a piece of stock. But I don't think that's the best way. The grain direction of the spline would end up the same direction as the joint. For greater strength it's better if the grain direction of the spline runs *perpendicular* to the joint line.

To cut splines with the grain running perpendicular to the joint line I use a two-step technique; see Step 5. By cutting the spline off the end of a piece of stock you'll actually end up with a spline that's wider than it is long. And that's exactly what you want.

One other thing. For the collector's cabinet, I cut the splines out of hard maple to match the doors. Then the spline almost disappears once the doors are glued up.

But sometimes I want to use the spline as a decorative accent. For those situations, I will use a contrasting wood such as the walnut spline in the photos shown above.

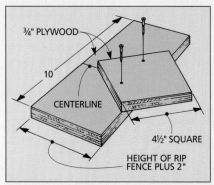

1 Cut a piece of ³/₄" plywood for the jig 10" long and to the height of your table saw's rip fence plus 2". Next, center a square piece diagonally on the jig and screw it down.

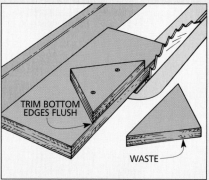

2 Raise the saw blade and set the rip fence so the angled piece will be trimmed flush with the bottom edge of the jig. Then push the whole jig through the saw and let the waste fall away.

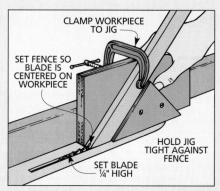

3 Clamp the workpiece to the jig and set the blade to cut a ¹/₄"-deep kerf. Holding the jig tight against the fence, adjust the fence so the blade is centered on the workpiece. Then cut a kerf.

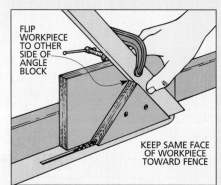

4 To kerf the other end, flip the piece over and clamp it to the other side of the angled support block. Keep the same face of the workpiece against the jig so the kerfs will all align.

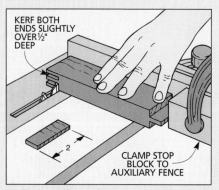

5 To cut the splines, raise the blade over ¹/₂" high, stand the workpiece on end, and kerf both ends. Then trim off the splines using a miter gauge and stop block.

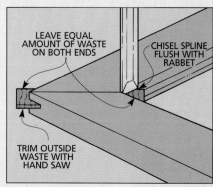

6 Glue the splines in place so equal amounts stick out either side. Trim off the outside end with a hand saw and sand flush. Use a chisel to trim the inside flush with the rabbet.

SCANDINAVIAN CORNER CABINET

Fitting a cabinet tightly into a corner can be a challenge. Especially if the corner isn't perfectly square. The design of this cabinet makes it easy to fit and hang.

This corner cabinet is reminiscent of cabinets found in rural Scandinavian homes. Since these were utilitarian cabinets, they were often made of the least expensive lumber — native pine. The joinery was equally simple and straightforward — butt joints held together with nails.

WOOD. I followed with tradition and made my cabinet out of pine: clear, quartersawn, $3/4$"-thick Ponderosa pine.

JOINERY. However, I couldn't bring myself to using butt joints and nails. Instead, I joined the main pieces with tongue and groove joints. The challenge was cutting the joints accurate and tight. With all the angles on a project like this, if the joinery doesn't fit tight, the gaps will be noticeable.

FITTING A CORNER. The other challenge was to design the project to hang and fit into a corner — even a corner that's a little out of square. The answer came in lapping the sides over the back so only the edge of the sides come in contact with the wall. In addition, there's a hidden hanging bracket that "bridges" over the point where the two walls of a room come together.

FINISH. I finished the cabinet with exterior urethane varnish. (It's yellowish, so the pine took on instant age.)

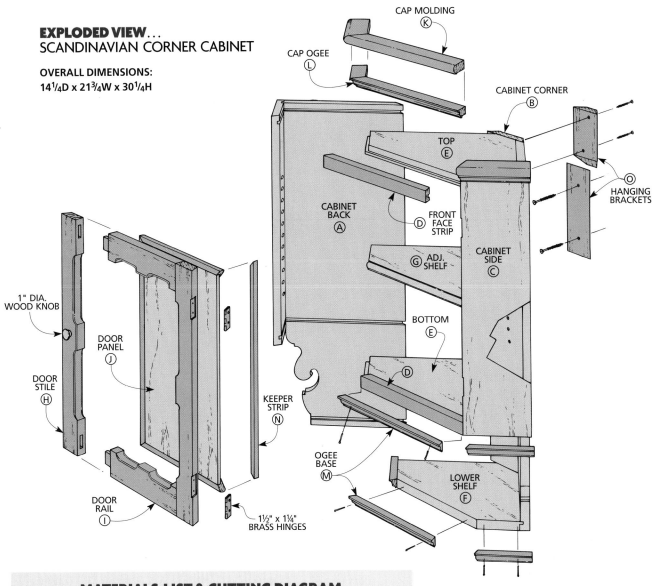

EXPLODED VIEW...
SCANDINAVIAN CORNER CABINET

OVERALL DIMENSIONS:
$14\frac{1}{4}$D x $21\frac{3}{4}$W x $30\frac{1}{4}$H

CAP MOLDING
K

CAP OGEE
L

CABINET CORNER
B

TOP
E

CABINET BACK
A

FRONT FACE STRIP
D

ADJ. SHELF
G

CABINET SIDE
C

HANGING BRACKETS
O

1" DIA. WOOD KNOB

DOOR PANEL
J

DOOR STILE
H

KEEPER STRIP
N

BOTTOM
E

DOOR RAIL
I

$1\frac{1}{2}$" x $1\frac{1}{4}$" BRASS HINGES

OGEE BASE
M

LOWER SHELF
F

MATERIALS LIST & CUTTING DIAGRAM

WOOD

A Cab. Backs (2)	$\frac{3}{4}$ x $11\frac{1}{4}$ - 29
B Cab. Corner (1)	$\frac{3}{4}$ x $4\frac{5}{16}$ - 29
C Cab. Sides (2)	$\frac{3}{4}$ x $5\frac{1}{2}$ - $20\frac{1}{4}$
D Frt. Face Strips (2)	$\frac{3}{4}$ x 1 - cut to fit
E Top/Btm. Pcs. (2)	$\frac{3}{4}$ x $11\frac{1}{4}$ - 19
F Lower Shelf (1)	$\frac{3}{4}$ x $11\frac{1}{4}$ - 19
G Adj. Shelf (1)	$\frac{3}{4}$ x $10\frac{3}{16}$ - $17\frac{3}{4}$

H Door Stiles (2)	$\frac{3}{4}$ x 2 - $18\frac{1}{8}$
I Door Rails (2)	$\frac{3}{4}$ x 2 - $10\frac{3}{8}$
J Door Panel (1)	$\frac{1}{2}$ x $9\frac{3}{4}$ - $15\frac{3}{4}$
K Cap Moldings (3)	$\frac{3}{4}$ x 2 - cut to fit
L Cap Ogees (3)	$\frac{3}{4}$ x $1\frac{1}{2}$ - cut to fit
M Ogee Base (6)	$\frac{3}{4}$ x $\frac{5}{8}$ - cut to fit
N Keeper Strips (4)	$\frac{1}{2}$ x $\frac{5}{8}$ - cut to fit
O Hang. Bracket (1)	$\frac{3}{4}$ x $2\frac{3}{4}$ - 13 rough

$\frac{3}{4}$ x $7\frac{1}{4}$ - 72 (Two Boards @ 3.6 Bd. Ft. Each)
| A | A | |
O

$\frac{3}{4}$ x $7\frac{1}{4}$ - 72 (Two Boards @ 3.6 Bd. Ft. Each)
| E | E | G |

$\frac{3}{4}$ x $7\frac{1}{4}$ - 72 (3.6 Bd. Ft.)
| C | C | B |
| D | D | |

$\frac{3}{4}$ x $7\frac{1}{4}$ - 72 (3.6 Bd. Ft.)
| F | F | H | I |

$\frac{1}{2}$ x $7\frac{1}{4}$ - 36 (1.8 Sq. Ft.)
| N | J | J | N |

NOTE: CUT MOLDING PIECES (K, L, M) FROM WASTE AREAS.

HARDWARE SUPPLIES
(1 pr.) $1\frac{1}{2}$" x $1\frac{1}{4}$" Brass butt hinges
(1) 1"-dia. Wood knob
(1) $\frac{3}{8}$"-dia. x $1\frac{5}{8}$"-long Dowel
(3) $\frac{1}{4}$" Spoon-style shelf supports
(12) No. 8 x $1\frac{1}{2}$" Fh Woodscrews
(2) No. 8 x $1\frac{1}{4}$" Fh Woodscrews
(2) 3" Drywall screws
(14) 4d Finish nails
(30) 1" Brads

CABINET BACK PIECES

Since this is a corner cabinet, it's not shaped like conventional furniture or wall shelves. Dealing with the unusual shape of this cabinet forced me to come up with names for parts that made sense. The "back" of the cabinet is actually made up of three separate pieces. I call the two wide pieces that fit against the walls the cabinet backs (A). The narrow piece (between the back pieces) is called the cabinet corner (B); see Fig. 1.

BACK PIECES. To make the back pieces (A), begin by gluing up stock to make two solid panels about 30" long and 12" wide. When the glue dries, cut the panels to a finished length of 29".

CORNER PIECE. Next, cut the corner piece (B) to a rough width of 5" and a finished length of 29".

BEVELS AND GROOVES

After the three pieces are cut to length, bevels are ripped on the edges.

BEVEL BACKS. The *rear* edge on both back pieces (A) is ripped at 45° to create a finished width of $11^1/4$"; see Fig. 1. Then both sides of the corner piece (B) are beveled so its width is $4^5/16$".

When beveling these edges, it may seem that the bevels are all backwards from the way they should be cut. But note that the cabinet corner piece (B) will be lapped over the beveled edges of the back pieces (A); see Fig. 1a.

BEVEL SIDE PIECES. Next, cut two cabinet sides (C) to a rough width of 6" and final length of $20^1/4$"; see Fig. 1. The *front* edge of each of these two side pieces is also beveled, but this time at $22^1/2$°. Bevel rip each side piece so the finished width is $5^1/2$" ; see Fig. 1.

GROOVES IN SIDES. The side pieces have a vertical groove (see Fig. 2) that accepts a tongue cut on the back pieces later. This groove is cut on the inside face and is positioned so when the cabinet sides are joined to the backs, the edges overlap (about $1/4$"); see Fig. 3a.

This offset allows the edges of the sides to fit tight against the wall, even if the walls are out of square; refer to Fig. 16a on page 20.

FACE STRIPS

Next, I cut the front face strips (D) to size; see Fig. 4. Then a groove is cut on these pieces to join them to the cabinet's top and bottom.

These grooves are positioned using the stock to set the fence. To do this, position the fence so the distance between the *outside* edge of the blade and the fence is equal to the stock thickness; see Fig. 4.

DADOES AND HOLES

The next step is to cut three sets of dadoes on the backs (A), corner piece (B), and sides (C). These dadoes are used to join these pieces to the cabinet's top, bottom and lower shelf; refer to the Exploded View.

TOP/BOTTOM DADOES. To position the top and bottom dadoes, leave the fence set up in the same position as it was for cutting the groove in the face strips. Then cut across all five pieces.

MIDDLE DADOES. Another set of

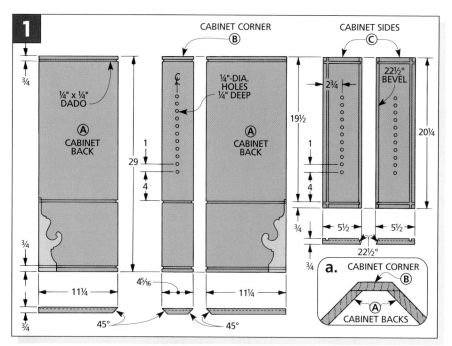

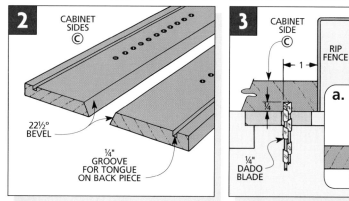

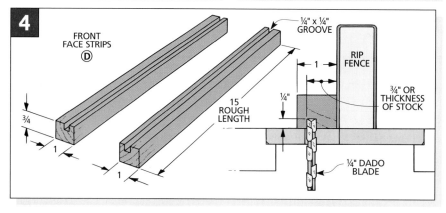

dadoes is cut across the backs (A) and corner piece (B) to join to the cabinet's bottom. Positioning these dadoes is a little tricky. They have to be positioned so they align exactly with the bottom dadoes on the two cabinet sides (C).

I found the best way to do this was to use a cabinet side (C) as a gauge to position the rip fence. First, butt one end of the side piece against the fence. Then

adjust the fence until the dado blade is precisely aligned with the bottom dado.

SHELF SUPPORT HOLES. Before going on to making the other parts of the case, holes are drilled in the corner piece (B) and cabinet sides (C) that will be used later for supports for the adjustable middle shelf; see locations in Fig. 1 (It's a lot easier to drill these holes now before the case is assembled.)

LAY OUT AND CUT SHELVES

After the outside case parts are complete, the cabinet's top, bottom, and shelves can be made. So all the angles came out the same, I began by making the top and bottom (both E), and lower shelf (F) all the same size.

LAYOUT. Begin by gluing stock to make three blanks 11¼" by 19". Then mark a centerline across each piece; see Fig. 5.

The centerline is used to lay out the shape of each piece. First mark the front and back corners working off the centerline; see Fig. 5. Then use a combination square to strike a 45° line from each mark on the front edge; see Fig. 6. Then mark a point along these diagonals 4½" from the front edge.

Now connect the marks on the back edge with the marks just made; see Fig. 7.

CUT TO SIZE. Next the pieces can be cut to size. The first cuts form the angled backs. I used the miter gauge set at 45° with a long auxiliary fence to make these cuts; see Fig. 8. Clamp a block to the fence to keep the workpiece from shifting.

After making the first cut, flip the blank end for end, keeping the same edge against the auxiliary fence. And remove the waste on the other back edge. Then repeat the process with the other blanks.

Now the small corners that will fit into the sides can be cut. For this I used the rip fence on my saw as a stop and guide; see Fig. 11. Again, make two cuts on each blank.

CUT TONGUES

The next step is making the tongues that will fit in the dadoes previously cut in the cabinet back and side pieces. These tongues are formed by using a ¼" dado blade to cut rabbets on the top, bottom, and lower shelf; see Fig. 10.

FENCE SPACER. To cut the tongues, I began by sticking a ¼" hardboard spacer to the rip fence with double-sided carpet tape. This keeps the dado blade from cutting the fence itself. Then I slid the fence and spacer over until the dado teeth barely rubbed the hardboard; see Fig. 10.

TONGUE THICKNESS. The tongues need to be cut ¼" thick to fit the ¼" dadoes in the cabinet sides and backs. To set the thickness, raise the dado blade slightly less than ½" and make a practice cut on a piece of scrap of the same thickness. Keep raising the blade a little at a time until the tongue left on the scrap fits snugly into the dado.

FORM TONGUES. I made tongues all the way around all three blanks because they're all identical at this time; see Fig. 11. (The front and side edges on the shelf will be cut away; refer to Fig. 14.)

BACK TONGUES. While the table saw is set up, tongues can be formed on the two cabinet backs (A) to fit the grooves in the cabinet sides (C). (Note: The tongue is formed on the same face as the long point of the bevel; see End View Detail in Fig. 13.)

DECORATIVE PROFILE

The next step is cutting the decorative profile on the lower end of the two cabinet backs (A). I found it easiest to make a template from a piece of ⅛" hardboard to trace around when drawing this profile on these two pieces.

MAKE TEMPLATE. To make the template, begin by laying out a 1" grid. Then make the profile by drawing circles with a compass and drilling out wherever possible; see Fig. 12. Then cut out the remaining areas with a band saw or sabre saw and sand the profile smooth.

POSITION PROFILE. To position the profile, align the bottom edge of the template with the bottom edge of the cabinet back (A), and the front edge against the edge with the tongues. Then trace around the template with a pencil. Finally, cut just outside the lines and sand up to the lines with a drum sander.

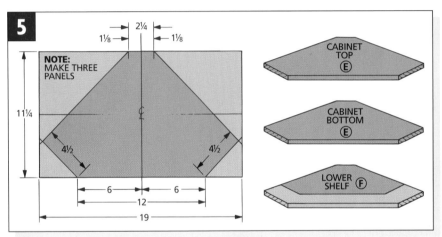

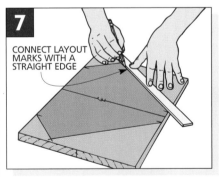

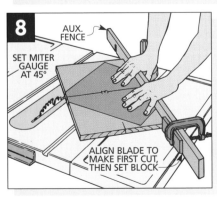

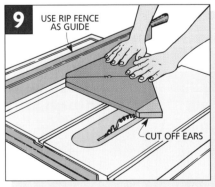

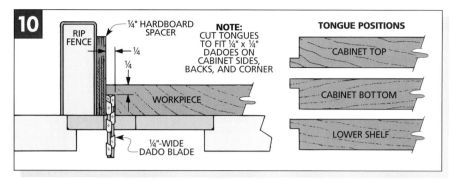

10

¼" HARDBOARD SPACER

RIP FENCE

¼

¼

WORKPIECE

NOTE: CUT TONGUES TO FIT ¼" x ¼" DADOES ON CABINET SIDES, BACKS, AND CORNER

¼"-WIDE DADO BLADE

TONGUE POSITIONS

CABINET TOP

CABINET BOTTOM

LOWER SHELF

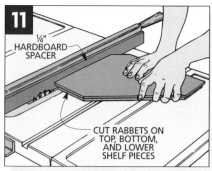

11

¼" HARDBOARD SPACER

CUT RABBETS ON TOP, BOTTOM, AND LOWER SHELF PIECES

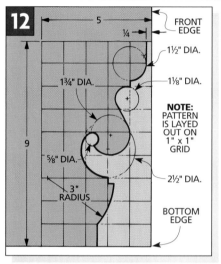

12

5

¼

FRONT EDGE

1½" DIA.

1⅛" DIA.

1¾" DIA.

NOTE: PATTERN IS LAYED OUT ON 1" x 1" GRID

9

⅝" DIA.

2½" DIA.

3" RADIUS

BOTTOM EDGE

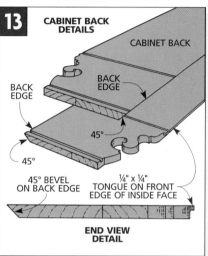

13

CABINET BACK DETAILS

CABINET BACK

BACK EDGE

BACK EDGE

45°

45°

45° BEVEL ON BACK EDGE

¼" x ¼" TONGUE ON FRONT EDGE OF INSIDE FACE

END VIEW DETAIL

LOWER SHELF

After the profiles are cut out, the lower shelf can be cut to size. Since the front edge of the profile determines the actual size of the shelf, first dry assemble the cabinet.

SCREW TOGETHER. To hold the cabinet together, I drove a single screw centered on the back pieces and the corner piece; see Fig. 14. (Don't screw in the shelf yet.)

LOWER SHELF. Now the lower shelf can be marked to be cut. Begin by pushing it into position and make a mark on the front edges of the shelf right at the edges of the profiles; see Fig. 14. Next, square out lines from these marks and mark a point 3¾" from the edge. Then connect these points and cut the shelf to shape.

ASSEMBLY

With all of the main case pieces completed, the case can be assembled.

I started by gluing and screwing the top, bottom and shelf to the cabinet backs; see Fig. 14. Then I added the cabinet sides and the corner piece.

ADD FACE STRIPS

After all of the main pieces have been assembled, there are two more pieces to add — the front face strips (D). These frame the top and bottom of the door opening. (Note: They were cut to *rough* length back on page 17, Fig. 4.)

CUT TO LENGTH. To cut these pieces to finished length, start by cutting a 22½° miter off *one* end of each piece. Then "sneak up" on the other end (also a 22½° miter cut), until the strip fits perfectly between the cabinet sides; see Top View in Fig. 14.

GLUE IN PLACE. Once the pieces fit, they can be glued onto the tongue on the front of the cabinet top and bottom.

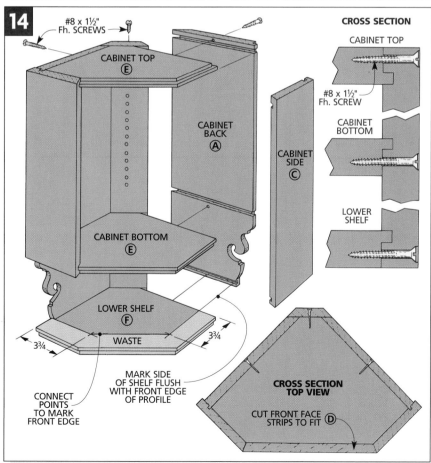

14

#8 x 1½" Fh. SCREWS

CABINET TOP (E)

CABINET BACK (A)

CABINET BOTTOM (E)

LOWER SHELF (F)

CONNECT POINTS TO MARK FRONT EDGE

3¾

WASTE

3¾

MARK SIDE OF SHELF FLUSH WITH FRONT EDGE OF PROFILE

CABINET SIDE (C)

CROSS SECTION

CABINET TOP

#8 x 1½" Fh. SCREW

CABINET BOTTOM

LOWER SHELF

CROSS SECTION TOP VIEW

CUT FRONT FACE STRIPS TO FIT (D)

ADJUSTABLE SHELF

With the cabinet done, I next made an adjustable shelf (G) to fit inside the cabinet. This shelf sits on three "spoon-style" shelf supports.

To determine the size of the adjustable shelf, measure the inside dimensions of the case. Then, to allow for clearance, subtract $1/8$" from these measurements; see Fig. 15. At the front of the shelf, subtract $5/8$" from the depth of the cabinet for the door panel that sticks out behind the back of the door; refer to Fig. 25.

Shop Note: To check out my measurements, I quickly cut a "prototype" shelf out of a piece of cardboard to make sure it fit.

Once the measurements are determined, build up a blank and cut it to size using the same technique used to make the other shelves; refer to Figs. 8 and 9.

PROFILE EDGE. After the adjustable shelf was cut to size, I routed a profile on the front edge using a $1/4$" roundover bit on the router table; see Fig. 15.

HANGING BRACKET

The cabinet hangs on the wall with a hidden "hook and bracket" hanger (O).

Begin making the hanger by bevel ripping both edges of a piece of stock so the width between the points of the bevels is the same as the back of the cabinet; see Fig. 16.

Next, cut the piece into two sections with the saw set at 45° to form the hook and bracket.

Now glue and screw the upper section (hook) to the cabinet. Finally, screw the lower section (bracket) into the corner studs of the wall with 3"-long drywall screws; see Fig. 16a.

THE DOOR FRAME

With the cabinet case complete, I went about making the door. The door frame consists of two stiles and two rails joined with mortises and tenons.

Begin by ripping all four pieces 2" wide; see Fig. 17. Then cut the rails (I) $10^3/8$" long. And cut the stiles (H) $1/8$" less than the opening between the top and bottom facing strips (D) (in my case, $18^1/8$") .

JOINTS. After cutting the stock to size, cut $1/4$"-wide centered mortises $1/2$" from both ends of the stiles, see Figs. 17 and 18. Then form matching tenons on the ends of the rails.

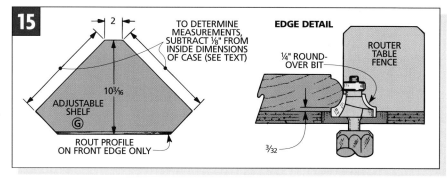

15 ADJUSTABLE SHELF (G) — 2 — $10^3/16$ — TO DETERMINE MEASUREMENTS, SUBTRACT $1/8$" FROM INSIDE DIMENSIONS OF CASE (SEE TEXT) — ROUT PROFILE ON FRONT EDGE ONLY

EDGE DETAIL — $1/4$" ROUNDOVER BIT — ROUTER TABLE FENCE — $3/32$

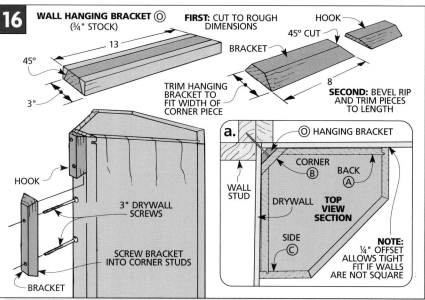

16 WALL HANGING BRACKET (O) ($3/4$" STOCK) — FIRST: CUT TO ROUGH DIMENSIONS — HOOK — 45° CUT — BRACKET — SECOND: BEVEL RIP AND TRIM PIECES TO LENGTH — 13 — 45° — 3" — 8 — TRIM HANGING BRACKET TO FIT WIDTH OF CORNER PIECE — HOOK — 3" DRYWALL SCREWS — SCREW BRACKET INTO CORNER STUDS — BRACKET

a. HANGING BRACKET — CORNER (B) — BACK (A) — WALL STUD — DRYWALL — TOP VIEW SECTION — SIDE (C) — NOTE: $1/4$" OFFSET ALLOWS TIGHT FIT IF WALLS ARE NOT SQUARE

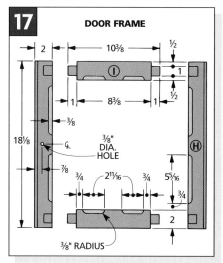

17 DOOR FRAME — 2 — $10^3/8$ — $1/2$ — 1 — $1/2$ — 1 — $8^3/8$ — 1 — (I) — $3/8$ — $18^1/8$ — C — $7/8$ — $3/4$ — $2^{11}/16$ — $3/4$ — $5^5/16$ — $3/4$ — 2 — (H) — $3/8$" DIA. HOLE — $3/8$" RADIUS

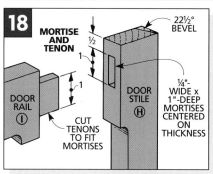

18 MORTISE AND TENON — $1/2$ — 1 — 1 — 1 — $22^1/2$° BEVEL — DOOR RAIL (I) — CUT TENONS TO FIT MORTISES — DOOR STILE (H) — $1/4$"-WIDE x 1"-DEEP MORTISES CENTERED ON THICKNESS

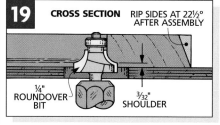

19 CROSS SECTION — RIP SIDES AT $22^1/2$° AFTER ASSEMBLY — $1/4$" ROUNDOVER BIT — $3/32$" SHOULDER

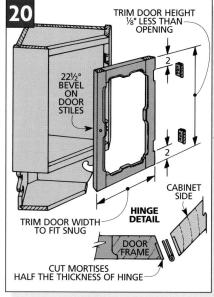

20 TRIM DOOR HEIGHT $1/8$" LESS THAN OPENING — 2 — 2 — $22^1/2$° BEVEL ON DOOR STILES — CABINET SIDE — HINGE DETAIL — TRIM DOOR WIDTH TO FIT SNUG — DOOR FRAME — CUT MORTISES HALF THE THICKNESS OF HINGE

PROFILE. Before assembly, cut out a double scalloped profile on the inside edges of the door frame parts; see Fig. 17. Then, glue the door frame together.

ROUT EDGES. To soften the scallops, I routed a profile with a $1/4$" roundover bit on the router table; see Fig. 19.

Note: When routing these edges, be careful not to "slip" out of the curved end of the scallop. The inside corners of the door frame should be left with square edges to contrast with the routed edge; refer to the photo on page 15.

TRIM TO SIZE. To fit the frame to the *height* of the opening in the case, trim the outside edges of the rails until the door fits between the face pieces with $1/16$" to spare on both ends; see Fig. 20.

To fit the frame to the *width* of the opening, begin by ripping a $22^1/2°$ bevel off each stile, leaving the door a little oversized. Then, sneak in on the cuts until the face of the door frame fits flush with the beveled edges on the sides of the cabinet.

HINGES. When the door fits its opening, mortise the door frame and the front edge of the cabinet side to accept two $1^1/2$" x $1^1/4$" hinges; see the Hinge Detail in Fig. 20.

DOOR LATCH

Before fitting the panel in the door frame, I fitted the latch.

TINKER TOY. The latch I used looks like a Tinker Toy but works great. The $3/8$" dowel shaft that goes through the door is glued into a wooden knob on one end and has a slot for a flat latch vane on the other; refer to Fig. 23.

KNOB. To make the knob work, I bored a hole in a 1"-dia. wood knob to fit the dowel shaft; see Fig. 21.

SLOT JIG. After gluing a short dowel into the knob, I used a simple jig to slot the other end of the shaft; see Fig. 22. To make this jig, begin by marking a centerline on a $1^1/2$"-wide piece of scrap. Next, drill a $3/8$" hole through the scrap about 1" from the end on the centerline.

CUT SLOT. To cut the slot, raise the saw blade so it projects just $1/2$" above the table. Next, insert the dowel into the hole so the end is flush with the bottom of the jig. Then adjust the saw fence so the blade is centered on the centerline, and push the jig through the blade.

LATCH VANE. To make the latch vane, rip a thin scrap of wood to fit the slot (about $1/8$" thick). Next, cut it with a

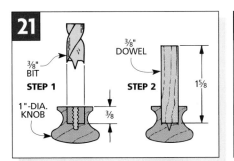

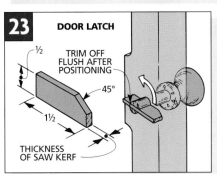

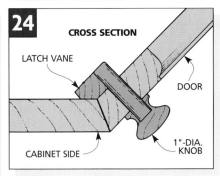

hand saw $1/2$" wide and $1^1/2$" long. Then cut off one corner at 45°; see Fig. 23.

FIT LATCH. Now the vane is fitted to hold the door shut. To do this, close the door and slide the vane in the slot until the angled corner of the vane fits in the inside corner of the cabinet; see Fig. 24. Then glue in the vane and trim off the excess flush with the dowel.

PANEL

Now the door frame is ready for the panel (J). In keeping with the simplicity of the cabinet, this panel is mounted to the back of the door frame (rather than set into grooves); see Fig. 25.

CUT TO SIZE. To make the panel, start by gluing up a blank from $1/2$" stock. Then, to determine the final

dimensions, measure the distances between the bottoms of the scallops on the frames and add $1/4$" in each direction; see Fig. 25.

RABBET EDGES. The panel is held by rabbeted strips; see Fig. 25a. Begin by rabbeting the edge of the panel to leave a $1/4$" x $1/4$" tongue around the edge.

KEEPER STRIPS. To make the keeper strips (N), cut a $1/4$" x $1/4$" rabbet along both edges of a $1/2$"-thick x 2"-wide blank. Next, rip $5/8$"-wide strips off each edge of the blank. Then round over the outside edges with a $1/4$" roundover bit; see Fig. 25a.

Next, miter the ends of the strips for a tight fit around the panels. Then position the panel and nail through the keeper strips with 1"-long brads to secure the panel in place; see Fig. 25a. Finally, mount the door in the cabinet.

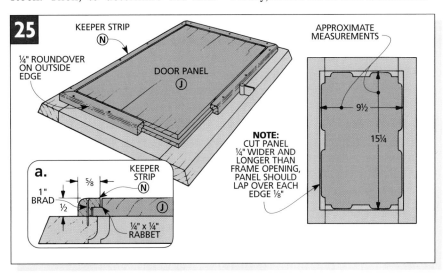

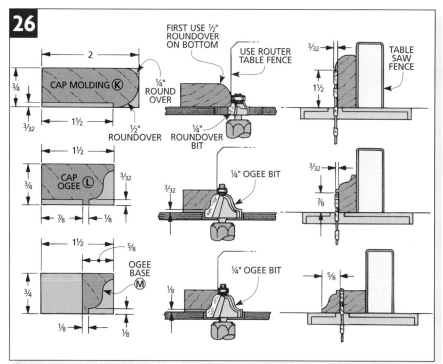

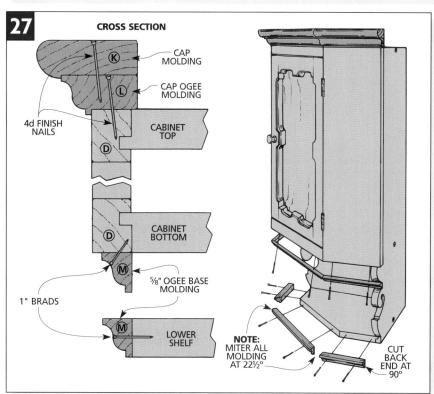

TRIM MOLDING

After the door panel was in place I made trim molding for the top and bottom of the cabinet and front of the lower shelf.

SHAPE PROFILES. Begin by using the router table to shape the profiles on blank stock; see Fig. 26. Next, use the saw to form the shallow rabbets where the molding pieces overlap. Then cut them to final width and miter to length.

ATTACH TRIM. Now the moldings can be glued to the case. I drove two nails through each strip to act as clamps while the glue dried; see Fig. 27.

Shop Note: To conceal the nail holes, I "blind nailed" the brads; for more information, see the box at right. ∎

Blind Nailing

One of the problems of using nails in a project is how to cover the nail holes. I was faced with this problem when fastening the molding to the Scandinavian corner cabinet.

The easy solution is to drive in the brad, countersink it, and fill the top of the hole with plastic wood putty. It's quick, but getting an exact color match with the wood is difficult.

There's another method to hide the nails that has been used by finish carpenters for years — blind nailing. To do this you lift up a chip, set the nail, and glue the chip back in place.

To lift the chip, there's a special tool available called a "blind nailer." It looks like a miniature plane that holds a small chisel for a blade.

If you're careful you can do the same thing with a small chisel.

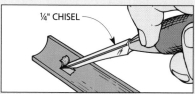

1 *With bevel down, wiggle chisel lightly forward and lift up a chip.*

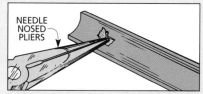

2 *Grip brad with pliers and tap it in with tack hammer and nail set.*

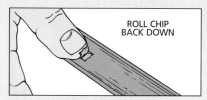

3 *Spread glue under chip with toothpick and roll down with thumb.*

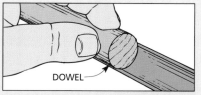

4 *Hold chip down with dowel a few minutes until the glue sets.*

COUNTRY PIE SAFE

It's brand new, but it looks old. That's the challenge in building this "new" antique with square nails and punched tin panels.

There were a lot of questions to consider as I started building this pie safe. The main attraction is the tin panels. But how do you punch the design in the tin?

What wood should be used? Pine, knotty or clear? Should it be distressed and finished to look old? Since the cab-inet is nailed together, it would be nice to use old square nails, but where can you get them?

And the most important question: Who will bake pies to fill the shelves?

I've managed to answer most of these questions on the following pages. (I'm still working on the pies.)

One of the first decisions was to build the pie safe out of No. 2 common pine. It had enough knots and defects to give the project a little "character." I tried to choose straight pieces, but I still let it sit in the shop a couple of weeks before I started working on it. Then I cut out any warped sections.

EXPLODED VIEW

OVERALL DIMENSIONS:
39¹⁄₂W x 13³⁄₄D x 54³⁄₄H

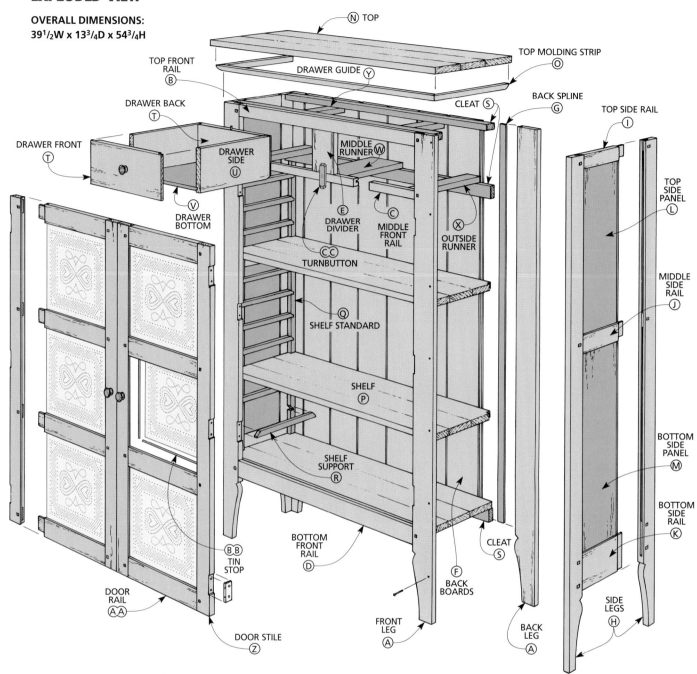

TOP Ⓝ

TOP FRONT RAIL Ⓑ

DRAWER GUIDE Ⓨ

TOP MOLDING STRIP Ⓞ

DRAWER BACK Ⓣ

BACK SPLINE Ⓖ

CLEAT Ⓢ

TOP SIDE RAIL Ⓘ

DRAWER FRONT Ⓣ

MIDDLE RUNNER Ⓦ

TOP SIDE PANEL Ⓛ

DRAWER SIDE Ⓤ

DRAWER BOTTOM Ⓥ

DRAWER DIVIDER Ⓔ

MIDDLE FRONT RAIL Ⓒ

OUTSIDE RUNNER Ⓧ

MIDDLE SIDE RAIL Ⓙ

TURNBUTTON Ⓒ Ⓒ

SHELF STANDARD Ⓠ

SHELF Ⓟ

BOTTOM SIDE PANEL Ⓜ

SHELF SUPPORT Ⓡ

BOTTOM SIDE RAIL Ⓚ

TIN STOP Ⓑ Ⓑ

BOTTOM FRONT RAIL Ⓓ

CLEAT Ⓢ

DOOR RAIL Ⓐ Ⓐ

BACK BOARDS Ⓕ

FRONT LEG Ⓐ

BACK LEG Ⓐ

SIDE LEGS Ⓗ

DOOR STILE Ⓩ

DRAWER DETAIL

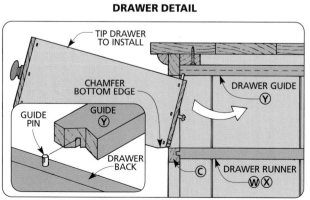

TIP DRAWER TO INSTALL

CHAMFER BOTTOM EDGE

GUIDE Ⓨ

GUIDE PIN

DRAWER BACK

DRAWER GUIDE Ⓨ

Ⓒ

DRAWER RUNNER Ⓦ Ⓧ

HINGE DETAIL

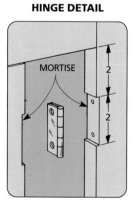

MORTISE

2

2

TURNBUTTON DETAIL

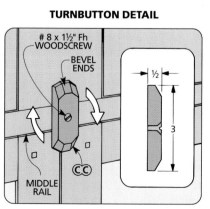

8 x 1½" Fh WOODSCREW

BEVEL ENDS

½

3

MIDDLE RAIL

Ⓒ Ⓒ

MATERIALS LIST

WOOD

A	Frt./Back Legs (4)	$\frac{3}{4}$ x 3 - 56 rough
B	Top Front Rail (1)	$\frac{3}{4}$ x $1\frac{1}{2}$ - 34
C	Mid. Front Rail (1)	$\frac{3}{4}$ x 1 - 34
D	Btm. Front Rail (1)	$\frac{3}{4}$ x 2 - 34
E	Drawer Divider (1)	$\frac{3}{4}$ x 4 - 5
F	Back Boards (6)	$\frac{3}{4}$ x $5\frac{1}{4}$ - 46
G	Back Splines (7)	$\frac{1}{4}$ x $\frac{3}{4}$ - 46
H	Side Legs (4)	$\frac{3}{4}$ x $2\frac{1}{4}$ - 56 rough
I	Top Side Rails (2)	$\frac{3}{4}$ x $1\frac{1}{2}$ - $9\frac{1}{2}$
J	Mid. Side Rails (2)	$\frac{3}{4}$ x 2 - $9\frac{1}{2}$
K	Btm. Side Rails (2)	$\frac{3}{4}$ x 4 - $9\frac{1}{2}$
L	Top Side Pnls. (2)	$\frac{1}{2}$ x $6\frac{7}{8}$ - $17\frac{7}{8}$
M	Btm. Side Pnls. (2)	$\frac{1}{2}$ x $6\frac{7}{8}$ - $21\frac{3}{8}$
N	Top (1)	$\frac{3}{4}$ x $13\frac{3}{4}$ - $39\frac{1}{2}$
O	Top Mold. Strip (1)	$\frac{3}{4}$ x $\frac{3}{4}$ - 72 rough
P	Shelves (3)	$\frac{3}{4}$ x $10\frac{7}{8}$ - $35\frac{1}{2}$
Q	Shelf Stands. (4)	$\frac{3}{4}$ x $\frac{1}{2}$ - 36 rough
R	Shelf Supports (4)	$\frac{3}{4}$ x $\frac{1}{2}$ - 11 rough
S	Cleats (5)	$\frac{3}{4}$ x $1\frac{1}{2}$ - $35\frac{1}{2}$
T	Drwr. Frt./Backs (4)	$\frac{3}{4}$ x 5 x $13\frac{1}{2}$
U	Drwr. Sides (4)	$\frac{3}{4}$ x 5 - 11
V	Drwr. Btms. (2)	$\frac{1}{2}$ x $10\frac{1}{2}$ - $12\frac{1}{2}$
W	Mid. Runner (1)	$\frac{3}{4}$ x $5\frac{1}{2}$ - $11\frac{1}{8}$
X	Outsd. Runners (2)	$\frac{3}{4}$ x 2 - $11\frac{1}{8}$
Y	Drwr. Guides (2)	$\frac{3}{4}$ x 2 - 11
Z	Door Stiles (4)	$\frac{3}{4}$ x 2 - $36\frac{1}{2}$
AA	Door Rails (8)	$\frac{3}{4}$ x 2 - $14\frac{1}{2}$
BB	Tin Stops	$\frac{1}{4}$ x $\frac{3}{8}$ - 30 ft.
CC	Turnbutton (1)	$\frac{1}{2}$ x $\frac{7}{8}$ - 3

HARDWARE SUPPLIES

(61) No. 8 x $1\frac{1}{4}$" Fh woodscrews
(12) No. 8 x 2" Fh woodscrews
(2) No. 8 x $\frac{3}{4}$" Rh screw
(1 lb.) 4d ($1\frac{1}{2}$" long) Square nails*
(72) $\frac{1}{2}$" Brads
(14) 1" Brads
(3 pr.) 2" x $1\frac{1}{2}$" Steel hinges w/screws
(6 pcs.) 10" x 14" Tin*
(4) $1\frac{1}{4}$-dia. Wooden knobs w/screws
* For Sources, see page 95

CUTTING DIAGRAM

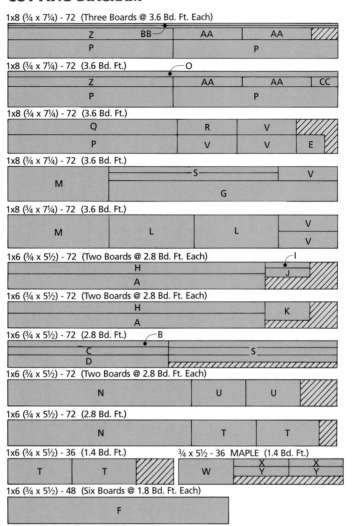

LEGS

I started building the pie safe by making the legs. They run the full height of the cabinet and also serve as the stiles (uprights) for the front, side, and back frames. Begin by cutting four front/back legs (A) from $\frac{3}{4}$"-thick stock, 3" wide and 56" long; see Fig. 1.

Each corner of the pie safe is actually two legs (a front or back leg and a side leg) nailed together; see Fig. 1. Since I wanted the width of the legs to appear the same from the front and the sides, cut the side legs (H) $\frac{3}{4}$" narrower ($2\frac{1}{4}$") than the front/back legs (A).

BOTTOM PROFILE. Next, a curved profile is cut on the bottom of all eight legs. I made a cardboard template (see Fig. 1) and then used it to lay out and cut the profile on all eight legs; see Fig. 1a.

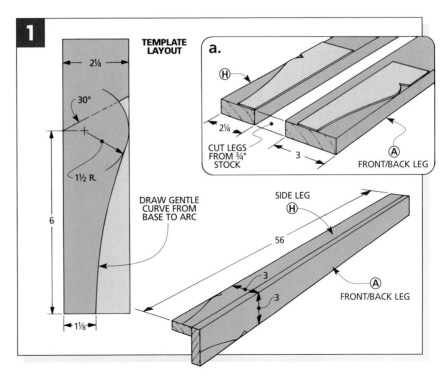

FRONT FRAME

Start building the front frame of the pie safe by ripping three rails to width: a top rail (B) $1\frac{1}{2}$" wide, a middle rail (C) 1" wide, and a bottom rail (D) 2" wide; see Fig. 2. All three rails are 34" long.

MORTISE AND TENONS. These rails are joined to the front legs (A) by cutting mortises along the *inside* edges of the front legs; see Fig. 2. Then cut matching tenons on the ends of all the rails to fit the mortises.

GROOVE MIDDLE RAIL. In order to be able to mount the drawer runners later, cut a $\frac{1}{4}$" groove on the *inside face* of the middle rail; see Fig. 2.

DRAWER DIVIDER. Next, dry assemble the frame and measure the distance between the top and middle rails. Then cut a 4"-wide drawer divider (E) to this length; see Fig. 2. Center the divider on the rails and screw it in place.

ASSEMBLY. Now the rails can be glued to the front legs. (I also added square wooden pegs through the joints; see the box on the opposite page.)

SIDE FRAMES

After the front frame is clamped up, you can begin work on the side frames.

RAILS. First rip the $1\frac{1}{2}$" top rails (I), the 2" middle rails (J), and the 4" bottom rails (K) to width; see Fig. 4. Then cut all six rails $9\frac{1}{2}$" long; see Fig. 3.

JOINERY. After the rails are cut to size, cut mortises on the inside edges of both side legs (H); see Fig. 3.

Note: Unlike on the front frame, the mortises on the side frames are narrower than the side rails. This is because the tenons are trimmed down that amount when grooves (for the panels) are cut in the rails; see Fig. 4.

Now cut the matching tenons on the rails. Then cut $\frac{1}{4}$" grooves on the edges of the rails; see Fig. 4.

GROOVES IN LEGS. There's one more set of $\frac{1}{4}$" x $\frac{1}{4}$" grooves to cut for the panels — on the *inside edge* of the side legs (H). The trick is to stop the groove before it cuts through the profile at the bottom of the legs. I used a pencil mark on the leg and a piece of tape on the table saw to mark where to stop the cut; see Fig. 5.

PANELS. Now the panels can be made. Start by gluing up enough $\frac{1}{2}$" stock (planed or resawn from $\frac{3}{4}$" stock) to make two top panels (L) and two bottom

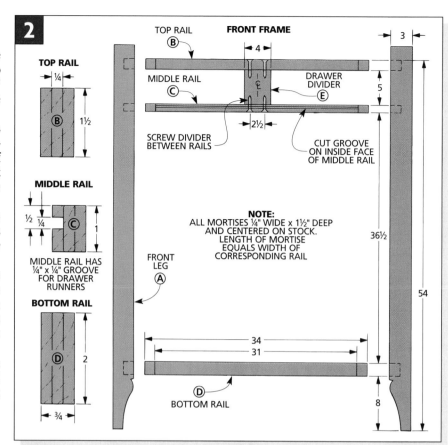

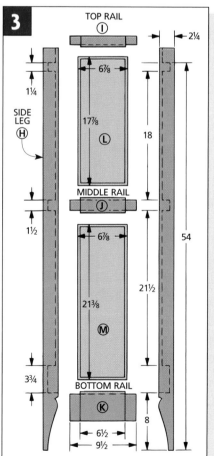

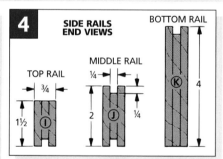

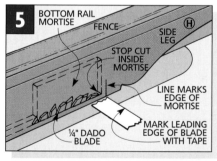

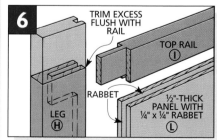

Square Pegs

On the pie safe, I added a square peg through each of the joints. Today's glues are strong enough that this isn't necessary, but it made the project a little more authentic. In the 19th century, the glue was of such poor quality that the joint needed more support — a peg or two to hold it together.

Not only are square pegs more authentic, but when a square peg is driven into a round hole, the corners wedge in tight and hold.

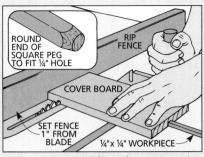

1 Round end of 1/4" x 1/4" stick with a pencil sharpener. With rip fence as a stop, place stick in groove in scrap cover board and safely cut to length.

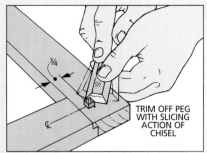

2 Drill 1/4" hole centered on mortise. (Don't drill out the back side.) Glue in peg with edge parallel to joint line. Saw off 1/8" proud and chisel flush.

---

panels (M). To allow for expansion, trim the panels 1/8" less than the distance between the grooves; see Fig. 3.

TONGUE. Next, to fit the panels into the grooves, cut a rabbet on the back edges of each panel to form a tongue along the front edge; see Fig. 6.

ASSEMBLY. After the rabbets are cut, the side frames can be glued and clamped square. Don't glue the panels into the grooves. (Just a dot of glue at the center of the top and bottom will keep the panel centered in the frame.)

After the side frames are assembled, cut the excess "ears" off the top ends of the side legs and front legs; see Fig. 6.

BACK ASSEMBLY

After the side frames were complete, I began work on the back. It's made from six boards connected between the two back legs. The problem is to connect the boards and still allow for expansion and contraction. I did this with cleats.

BACK BOARDS. The total width of all six back boards (F) together must equal the shoulder-to-shoulder distance of the front frame rails (31"). After I cut the boards so they added up to a total of 31", I trimmed an extra 1/16" off each board to allow for expansion. Then cut all the boards 46" long; see Fig. 7.

SPLINES. To align the boards for the back, I used 1/4" splines set into 3/8"-deep grooves cut in the edges of the boards; see Fig. 8.

After the grooves are cut, cut splines (G) to fit the grooves. Then glue the splines into one side of each board; see Fig. 8. (Don't glue the splines into adjoining edges or the boards won't be able to expand and contract.)

ASSEMBLE THE BACK. To assemble the back, space the pieces out evenly until the overall width of the back (including the legs) equals the width of the front frame (37"). Make sure that the bottom ends of the boards are up 8" from the bottom of the legs; see Fig. 7.

Next, cut two cleats (S) to hold the

back together. Cut them to length so they stop 3/4" from each side; see Fig. 9.

Screw (don't glue) the two cleats down across the assembly with two screws in each board to prevent racking; see Figs. 7 and 9.

When the back is assembled, cut the excess "ears" off the top; see Fig. 7.

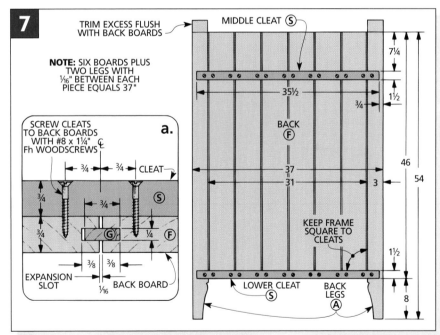

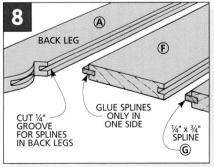

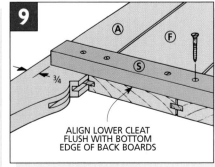

ASSEMBLING THE CABINET

Before assembling the cabinet, cut two more cleats (S), and screw them *on edge* to the inside of the front frame and the back assembly flush with the top; see Figs. 10 and 11. To support the bottom shelf, screw one more cleat to the inside of the front frame; see Fig. 12.

ASSEMBLY. Now the cabinet parts can be nailed together see Fig. 11. You could use standard 4d finishing nails, but I used square nails. (For sources of square nails, see page 95.). To prevent splitting when driving square nails, drill $1/8$" holes (every 8").

SHELVES. Once the cabinet is assembled, edge-glue enough $3/4$" stock to make three shelves (P) (one fixed and two adjustables). To allow for expansion, cut the shelves $1/8$" narrower than the inside depth of the cabinet; see Fig. 12. Then install the bottom shelf and nail it to the front cleat.

DRAWERS

To build the two drawers, cut four drawer front/backs (T) to the size of the drawer openings; see Fig 13. (Shop Note: After the drawers were assembled, I planed them slightly for clearance.) Next, cut four drawer sides (U) 11" long.

JOINERY. To join these pieces, I cut rabbets in the front/backs; see Fig. 13. I also cut grooves (for the bottom panel) in the front and side pieces.

BOTTOM. To make the drawer bottoms (V), I glued up $3/4$"-thick blanks and planed them down to $1/2$" thick. Then I cut a $1/4$" tongue on the front and sides.

ASSEMBLY. Once all the pieces are cut, glue and nail the front (T) to the sides (U). Then slide the bottom (V) into the grooves from the back. (Don't glue it in.)

The drawer back (T) sits on top of the bottom (V) and has to be cut to width. When it's cut, glue and nail it to the sides. Then, to hold the bottom in the grooves, tack a nail up into the back.

After the drawers are assembled, screw a roundhead screw into the back to act as a depth stop; see Fig. 13a.

DRAWER RUNNERS. The drawers ride on maple runners. Cut one middle runner (W) $5^1/2$" wide and two outside runners (X) 2" wide. The length equals the inside depth of the cabinet plus $1/8$".

To mount the runners, cut rabbets on the front end to produce a $1/4$"

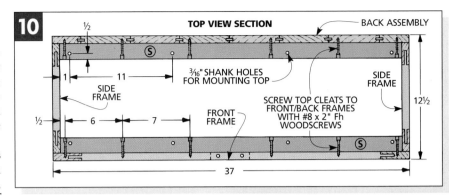

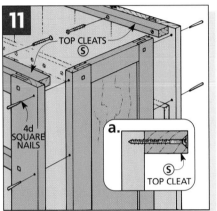

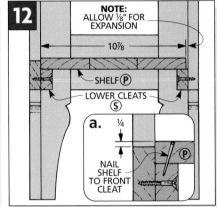

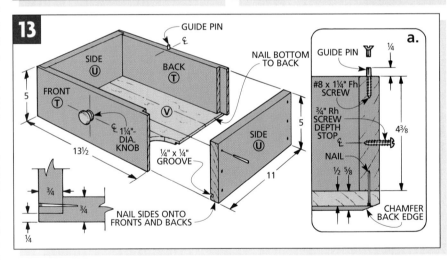

tongue; see Fig. 14c. Then slip the tongues in the groove in the middle front rail (C) and screw the back end down to the cleats; see Fig. 14.

DRAWER GUIDES. I've developed a drawer guide system that has a single maple guide (Y) mounted above each drawer. The guide has a groove (see Fig. 14b) to accept a guide pin made from a screw. This pin is screwed into the top of the drawer back; see Fig. 13a.

Before mounting the guides, plane a chamfer on the bottom back edge of the drawer sides so the drawers can be tipped into the opening; refer to the Drawer Detail on page 24.

Then to mount a drawer guide, hold the guide up under the top cleats and slide the drawer in. Then screw the back end of the guide in place.

Next pull the drawer until it's almost out of the cabinet and centered in the opening. Then screw the front of the guide in place.

CABINET TOP

Now the cabinet is ready for the top. Edge-glue the top (N) from three pieces of $3/4$"-thick stock and cut the blank $1^1/4$" wider and $2^1/2$" longer than the cabinet; see Fig. 14.

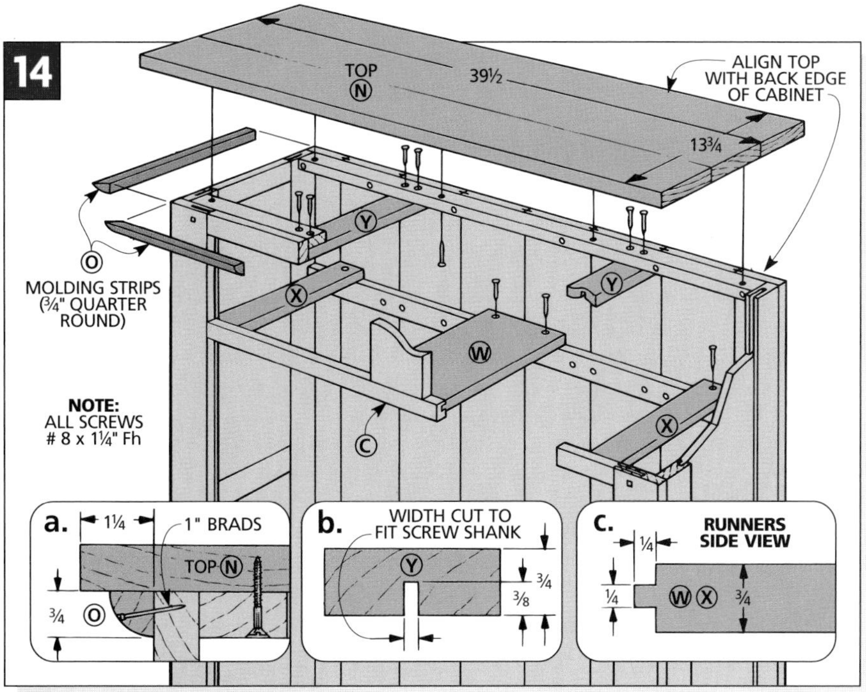
14
TOP
N
39½
ALIGN TOP WITH BACK EDGE OF CABINET
13¾
Y
Y
X
X
W
C
O
MOLDING STRIPS (¾" QUARTER ROUND)
NOTE: ALL SCREWS # 8 x 1¼" Fh
a.
1¼
1" BRADS
TOP N
¾
O
b.
WIDTH CUT TO FIT SCREW SHANK
Y
¾
⅜
c.
¼
RUNNERS SIDE VIEW
¼
W X
¾

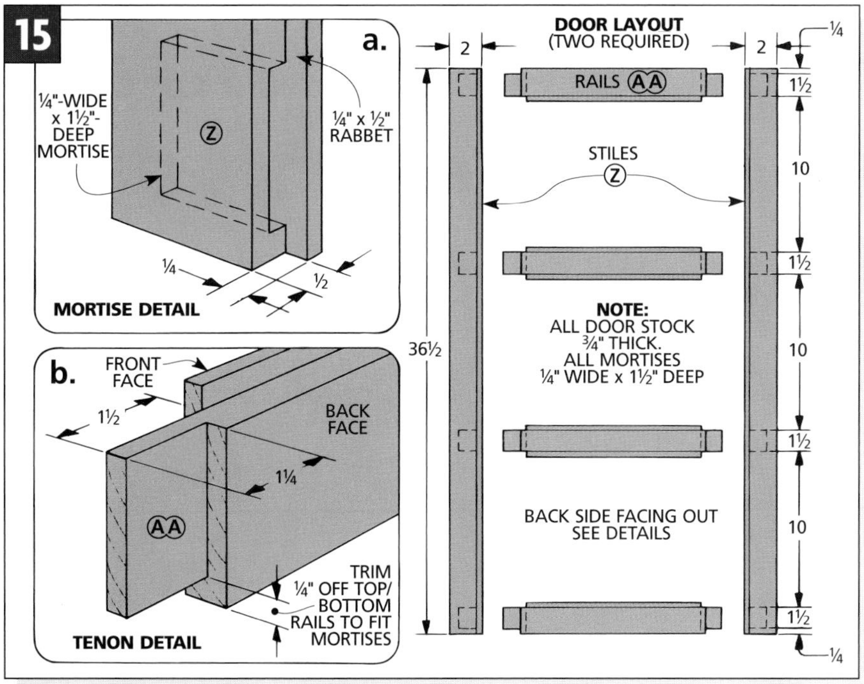
15
a.
¼"-WIDE x 1½"-DEEP MORTISE
Z
¼" x ½" RABBET
¼
½
MORTISE DETAIL
b.
FRONT FACE
1½
BACK FACE
1¼
AA
TRIM ¼" OFF TOP/ BOTTOM RAILS TO FIT MORTISES
TENON DETAIL
DOOR LAYOUT (TWO REQUIRED)
2
2
¼
RAILS AA
1½
STILES
Z
10
36½
1½
NOTE: ALL DOOR STOCK ¾" THICK. ALL MORTISES ¼" WIDE x 1½" DEEP
10
1½
BACK SIDE FACING OUT SEE DETAILS
10
1½
¼

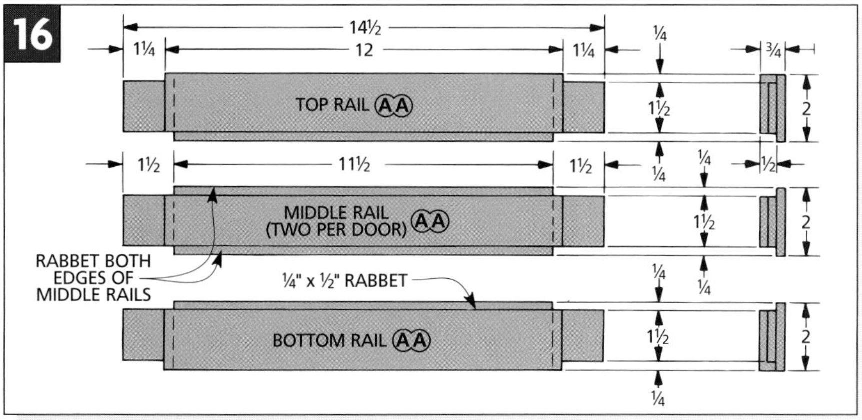
16
14½
1¼
12
1¼
¼
¾
TOP RAIL AA
1½
2
1½
11½
1½
¼
¼
½
MIDDLE RAIL (TWO PER DOOR) AA
1½
2
RABBET BOTH EDGES OF MIDDLE RAILS
¼" x ½" RABBET
¼
¼
BOTTOM RAIL AA
1½
2
¼

To attach the top, first drill shank holes through the top cleats; see hole locations in Fig. 10. Then center the top across the width of the cabinet and flush with the back, and screw (but don't glue) it down from the inside.

MOLDING. I also nailed on a $^3/_4$" quarter-round molding strip (O) under the top; see Figs. 14 and 14a. It's mitered at the front corners and cut flush at the back.

THE DOORS

The focal point of this whole cabinet is the doors with the punched tin panels.

STILES. To make the door frames, begin by cutting four door stiles (Z) to a width of 2" and to length to match the exact height of the cabinet opening ($36^1/_2$" in my case); see Fig. 15. (Shop Note: I usually find it easiest to cut the door parts to fit *tight* and then plane them down after assembly.)

After the stiles are cut to size, cut four mortises on the *inside* edge of each stile to accept the rails; see Fig. 15.

RAILS. To determine the length of the door rails (AA), measure one half the cabinet opening ($15^1/_2$"), subtract the width of two stiles (4") and add in the length of two $1^1/_2$"-long tenons (3"). In my case this total came to $14^1/_2$". Then cut eight rails to this length and 2" wide; see Fig. 16.

RABBETS. Before cutting the tenons on the rails, cut a $^1/_4$" x $^1/_2$" rabbet to hold the tin panels. These rabbets are cut on the back edge of the rails and on the stiles; see Figs. 15 and 16.

TENONS. Next, cut tenons on all of the rails. However, when the rabbet was cut on the back of the stiles, it created staggered shoulders; see Fig. 15a. So, cut the tenon's shoulder on the *front* face $1^1/_2$" from the end. But the shoulder on the *back* face is cut only $1^1/_4$" from the end to allow the tenon to "fill in" the rabbet; see Fig. 15b.

ASSEMBLY. After the tenons fit the mortises, dry-assemble the doors and test fit them in the openings. If they fit, glue all the parts together. (Note: After assembly, I clamped the parts for about two minutes until the glue "grabbed" and then fit the doors into the opening to hold them until they dried.)

After the glue dries, remove each door and plane the edges to create a $^1/_{16}$" gap between the door and the frame and $^1/_8$" between the doors.

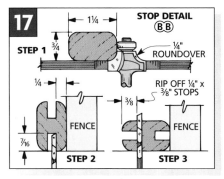

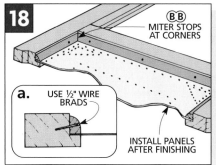

TIN PANELS AND HARDWARE

After the doors are planed to fit in the openings, the stops that hold the tin panels in place can be made.

STOPS. To make the tin stops (BB), round over all four edges of a piece of $^3/_4$" stock; see Step 1, Fig. 17. Then make four cuts to form an "H-shaped" block; see Step 2. Finally, rotate the block on its side and trim off the tin stops; see Step 3.

After the tin stop molding was made, I cut the tin to fit into the openings. (For more information on punching and aging the tin; see pages 31-32.) Once the tin is in place, the stops can be mitered to fit; see Fig. 18. (I didn't install the tin until after the finish was applied.)

HINGES AND KNOBS. Now the doors are mounted to the front frame with three butt hinges on each door. Cut the mortises for the hinges in the door frame and front frame; refer to the Hinge Detail on page 24. Also, drill the holes for $1^1/_4$" dia. wooden door knobs.

TURNBUTTON. The doors are held closed with a turnbutton (CC) cut from a piece of $^1/_2$" stock; refer to the Turnbutton Detail on page 24. Pare bevels on the ends of the turnbutton with a chisel, and then screw it to the middle rail so when it's turned it holds both doors closed.

SHELVES

The last step on the pie safe is to install the two adjustable shelves. I decided to use an old-fashioned notched system to hold the shelves; see Fig. 19.

STANDARDS. I cut all four standards (Q) from one 3" wide by 36" (rough length) board; see Fig. 19a. (This keeps the notches in all four shelf standards aligned.) Lay out the notches 3" apart on the edge of the board, and make 45° angled, $^1/_2$"-deep cuts.

Then make 90° cuts so they meet the ends of the angled cuts. (If the two cuts

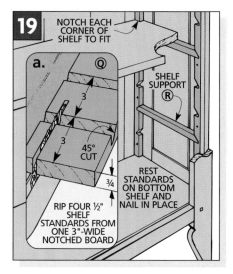

don't meet perfectly, clean out the bottom of the notch with a chisel.)

To cut the workpiece to length, measure the distance from the bottom shelf to the bottom of the cleat below the drawers. Then cut it this length, and rip it into four standards; see Fig. 19a.

Nail each standard into a corner of the cabinet with the bottom end resting firmly on the bottom shelf; see Fig. 19.

SUPPORTS. Next, cut four shelf supports (R) with chamfered ends to fit the notches in the standards; see Fig. 19.

NOTCH SHELVES. Finally, notches are cut in the corners of the shelves to allow them to fit around the standards.

The only steps left are to distress the pie safe (if you want, see below), finish it, and install the tin panels. ∎

Distressing

When building this pie safe I decided I wanted it to look 100 years old, but as though it had a good life — a few nicks and rounded edges from wear. But I didn't want to do this by pushing it over a gravel driveway. The trick is asking yourself what kind of wear this piece might show after 100 years.

JOINTS. After that much time, the joints would probably be a little loose. To create the appearance of a gap in a mortise and tenon (but keep a strong joint), I sanded a *slight* round on the edges of the two matching pieces. This creates a shadow line that looks like a gap, see photo.

To create a gap on miters, I wasn't quite as careful when setting up the miter gauge to exactly 45° or clamping

the joint perfectly tight.

SANDING. When sanding, round corners and edges by hand so it looks like there has been some natural wear. Concentrate on the bottom third of the project. That's where years of a broom bumping against it or a dog chewing on it would be seen.

WORMHOLES. To make "wormholes," bend some fine wire into a wavy pattern and tap it into the wood until an impression is left.

DIRT. One way to make the project look "dirty" is to set the nails slightly below the surface of the wood. The stain that soaks in around the nail will look like a natural build-up of dirt.

Or try rubbing a little rottenstone or even fine dirt into the gouges and nail

holes, around the knobs and turnbutton, and along some of the edges.

CAUTION. Be careful and don't overdo the distressing though. It's a fine line, and too much looks phony.

TECHNIQUE . . . . *Punching Tin*

When I first started designing the pie safe I thought punching the tin would be the easiest and quickest part of the project. I found out it's not too difficult, but it isn't quick.

There are 1,343 holes in each panel of the "Hearts on a Blanket" design we used in our pie safe. It took a little over an hour to punch the first panel, but after developing a technique I was able to punch the remaining panels in about 45 minutes each.

Punching a panel is fun, but tedious work. Your hands, forearms, and eyes quickly tire. I found it easier to spread the task of punching the tin over a period of two or three days.

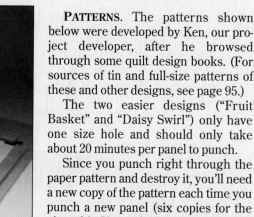

PATTERNS. The patterns shown below were developed by Ken, our project developer, after he browsed through some quilt design books. (For sources of tin and full-size patterns of these and other designs, see page 95.)

The two easier designs ("Fruit Basket" and "Daisy Swirl") only have one size hole and should only take about 20 minutes per panel to punch.

Since you punch right through the paper pattern and destroy it, you'll need a new copy of the pattern each time you punch a new panel (six copies for the pie safe). If you design your own pattern, photocopies can be made from your original.

Hearts on a Blanket

Fruit Basket

Daisy Swirl

Setting Up

After getting the patterns, the next step is fastening them to the tin.

PATTERN TO TIN. Start by aligning the pattern with the top edge of the tin and center it on the length. Then tape it down with masking tape; see Fig. 1. Because the 10" x 12" pattern is smaller

than the 10" x 14" tin, there will be 1" of waste on the sides to practice punching.

BACKING BOARD. The next step is to fasten the tin to a 12" x 16" backing board; see Fig. 2. To keep from punching into existing holes, I used a new 1/4" hardboard backing board for

each panel that I punched. Since hardboard is very consistent, it's easy to control the depth of the punches.

KEEPER STRIPS. To keep the tin from curling or moving while you punch, screw a 1/4" x 1" keeper strip along each side; see Fig. 2.

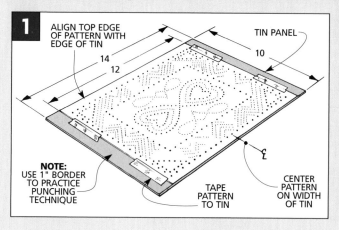

1
ALIGN TOP EDGE OF PATTERN WITH EDGE OF TIN
TIN PANEL
14
12
10
NOTE: USE 1" BORDER TO PRACTICE PUNCHING TECHNIQUE
TAPE PATTERN TO TIN
CENTER PATTERN ON WIDTH OF TIN

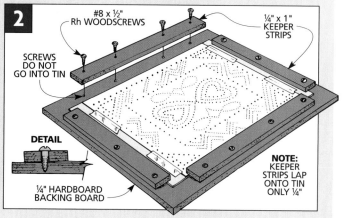

2
#8 x 1/2" Rh WOODSCREWS
1/4" x 1" KEEPER STRIPS
SCREWS DO NOT GO INTO TIN
DETAIL
1/4" HARDBOARD BACKING BOARD
NOTE: KEEPER STRIPS LAP ONTO TIN ONLY 1/4"

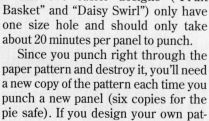

Punching the Tin

Once the tin is fastened to the backing board, you're ready to start punching.

PUNCHING TOOL. What's the best tool for punching? I tried some metal center punches, but the point angle was too flat to pierce the tin; see Fig. 3. I also tried a scratch awl. It punched the small holes, but I couldn't drive it deep enough to make the large holes.

To punch the tin for the pie safe, I used a Stanley scratch awl. It has a thick shaft that tapers quickly down to a point starting about $3/16$" from the end; see Fig. 3. That's the best shape for punching various size holes. An old nail set could also be ground down to this shape on a grinder.

To make the punching as easy as possible, sharpen your punching tool by spinning it against a grinder or honing it sharp on a stone. It should be sharp enough to easily pierce the tin.

PRACTICE. After the tool is sharp, practice punching in the border areas until you develop a technique that will consistently give you the correct size holes. The more complicated patterns have two different size holes; see Fig. 4.

The larger holes should be about $3/32$" in diameter. The smaller holes should be $1/32$" in diameter. If the pattern has only one size hole, $1/16$" is about right.

SMALL HOLES. To punch the small holes, grip the shaft of the awl with one hand and hold the point on the dot in the pattern. Then choke half way up the hammer handle with the other hand. (Note: I used a 16 oz. hammer.)

Now raise the hammer about six inches above the awl and drop it onto the awl. There shouldn't be any muscle behind it. If the awl is sharp enough, the point will pierce the tin and leave a hole about $1/32$" in diameter; see Fig. 4a.

LARGE HOLES. To produce the larger $3/32$"-dia. holes (Fig. 4b), you have to give the awl a firm blow. It's about like setting a nail with a nail set.

The trick in punching both size holes is developing some consistency. Before you actually punch the pattern, practice in the waste area until you can punch holes of a fairly consistent size (large or small). Don't worry if your holes vary a bit. It adds to the character of the piece if the holes vary slightly.

FLATTEN THE TIN. After all the holes are punched, remove the tin from the backing board and carefully flatten out any large, rolling bumps with your fingers. Don't cut off the borders yet. The borders serve as "handles" when you age the tin.

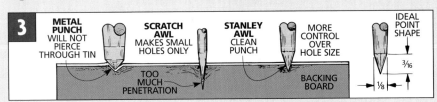

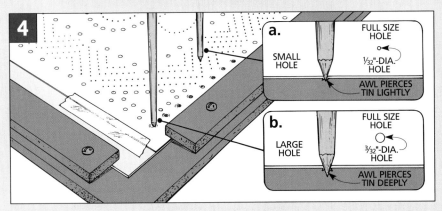

Aging the Tin

As it comes, the tin looks too new and shiny to fit into the antique look of the pie safe. To develop an "aged" appearance, the tin has to oxidize. (I also aged the steel hinges with this same method.)

WASH THE TIN. The first step in this process is to wash off any fingerprints or dirt with dishwashing detergent.

SOAKING TANK. Next, I made a soaking tank from 1x3's and a plastic garbage bag; see Fig. 5. Then I soaked the panels (two at a time) in a gallon of white vinegar.

To keep the tin panels from touching each other or the bottom, separate them with scraps of wood, see Fig. 5a. If the wood floats the panels, add some weight, but make sure the weight and spacers only touch the waste area.

The face side of the tin should face up in the tank. As the tin oxidizes, bub-

bles develop and float up under the bottom side leaving a blotchy surface.

RINSE. After the tin has soaked overnight, lift it out of the tank by the waste borders. Immediately rinse off the entire panel under running water, wiping off any residue with a soft rag.

Then, to prevent water spots, dry it immediately with a hair dryer or fan.

CUT TO SIZE. Once it's dry, cut off the waste with tin snips so the panel fits the opening and the design is centered.

PREVENTING RUST. Over time, the tin might rust from humidity. To keep it from rusting, seal the panels with a spray *matte* varnish. It's used by artists to seal acrylic and oil paintings and is available at art supply stores.

COUNTRY HUTCH

Knotty pine boards give this hutch an authentic "country" look.
Simple design and joinery make it fairly easy to build.

Around my shop, change is a daily routine. Originally, I planned to build this hutch from clear pine. That all changed at the lumberyard when I learned clear pine (C-select & better) now costs more than T-bone steak. So I made a change and used No. 2 common. Same wood, more knots, but a big difference in price.

KNOTS IN PINE. Knotty pine makes a country project look more interesting, but it also make building the project more interesting. Too many knots and the hutch would look like it was made from used pallets. For the best effect, I like to spend the time to lay out the pieces so the knots will be randomly spaced throughout the project.

FINISH. To finish the hutch, I wanted the look of aged pine. So I used a honey maple stain. But to avoid the blotches that can occur when staining pine, first I applied a stain controller (sometimes called "wood conditioner").

Once the stain dried, I applied a couple of coats of General Finishes' Royal Finish (urethane and oil mixture).

OVERALL DIMENSIONS:
80H x 50W x 18³/₄D

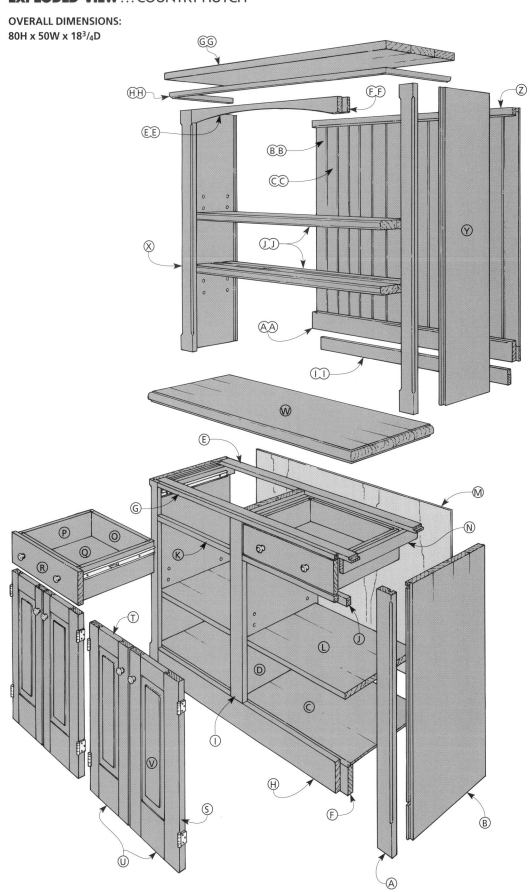

CUTTING DIAGRAM

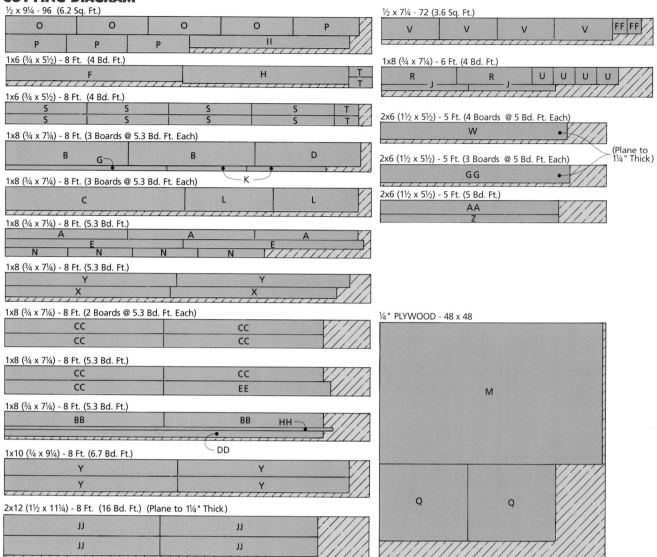

MATERIALS LIST

LOWER CABINET

A	Vertical Facings (2)	$3/4 \times 2^1/_2 - 32^3/_4$
B	Sides (2)	$3/4 \times 17^5/_8 - 32^3/_4$
C	Bottom Shelf (1)	$3/4 \times 17 - 47^1/_4$
D	Center Divider (1)	$3/4 \times 17 - 27^3/_4$
E	Stretchers (2)	$3/4 \times 2 - 47^1/_4$
F	Lower Backer (1)	$3/4 \times 4^1/_4 - 46^1/_2$
G	Upper Facing (1)	$3/4 \times 1 - 43$
H	Lower Facing (1)	$3/4 \times 4^1/_2 - 43$
I	Divider Facing (1)	$3/4 \times 2^1/_2 - 27^1/_4$
J	Middle Backers (2)	$3/4 \times 1^1/_2 - 22^7/_8$
K	Middle Facings (2)	$3/4 \times 1 - 20^1/_4$
L	Shelves (2)	$3/4 \times 16^7/_8 - 22^3/_4$
M	Cabinet Back (1)	$1/4$ ply - $47^1/_2 - 28^1/_2$
N	Drwr. Mtg. Rails (4)	$3/4 \times 2 - 17$
O	Drwr. Frts./Bks. (4)	$1/2 \times 4^3/_8 - 18^3/_4$
P	Drwr. Sides (4)	$1/2 \times 4^3/_8 - 16$
Q	Drwr. Bottoms (2)	$1/4$ ply - $18^3/_4 \times 15^1/_2$
R	False Drwr. Frts. (2)	$3/4 \times 4^3/_8 - 20^1/_8$

S	Door Stiles (8)	$3/4 \times 2^1/_2 - 21^5/_8$
T	Door Rails, Top (4)	$3/4 \times 2^1/_2 - 5^3/_4$
U	Door Rails, Bot. (4)	$3/4 \times 4^1/_2 - 5^3/_4$
V	Door Panels (4)	$1/2 \times 5^5/_8 - 15^1/_4$
W	Top (1)	$1^1/_4 \times 18^3/_4 - 49^1/_2$

UPPER CABINET

X	Vert. Facings (2)	$3/4 \times 2^1/_2 - 44^3/_4$
Y	Sides (2)	$3/4 \times 11^5/_8 - 44^3/_4$
Z	Upr. Back Rail (1)	$1^1/_2 \times 1^1/_2 - 47^1/_4$
AA	Lwr. Back Rail (1)	$1^1/_2 \times 3^1/_2 - 47^1/_4$
BB	Outs. Bck. Slts. (2)	$3/4 \times 3^7/_8 - 41^3/_{16}$
CC	Ins. Back Slats (11)	$3/4 \times 3^1/_2 - 41^3/_{16}$
DD	Splines (12)	$3/4 \times 1/4 - 41^3/_{16}$
EE	Valance (1)	$3/4 \times 3^1/_2 - 43$
FF	Screw Blocks (2)	$1/2 \times 3 - 3^1/_2$
GG	Top (1)	$1^1/_4 \times 13 - 50$
HH	Molding (1)	$3/4 \times 5/8 - 84$ rough
II	Connect. Cleat (1)	$1/2 \times 2^1/_2 - 44$
JJ	Shelves (2)	$1^1/_4 \times 10^3/_8 - 46^3/_8$

HARDWARE SUPPLIES

(38) No. 6 x 3/4" Fh woodscrews
(20) No. 8 x 1" Fh woodscrews
(44) No. 8 x 1 1/4" Fh woodscrews
(8) No. 8 x 1 1/2" Fh woodscrews
(26) No. 8 x 2" Fh woodscrews
(16) No. 8 x 2 1/2" Fh woodscrews
(8) 1 1/4" Birch knobs
(4 pr.) 2" x 1 3/8" Butt hinges
(4) Magnetic door catches
(16) 1/4" Spoon-style shelf supports
(2) Figure-8 fasteners
(2 pr.) 16" Full-extension drawer slides

LOWER CABINET

I started the hutch by building the lower cabinet. This starts out as a case with sides, a bottom shelf, and a divider.

Note: Most of this project is built from solid pine panels. So I started by gluing up enough boards for all five of the panels for the lower cabinet; see Figs. 1 and 2.

VERTICAL FACING STRIPS. While the glue is drying on the panels, a pair of vertical facing strips (A) can be cut to finished dimensions; see Fig. 1.

The facing strips are attached to the front edge of the side pieces. But rather than attaching them with a simple butt joint I decided to use a tongue and groove joint; see Fig. 1a. This helps keep the mating pieces in alignment during assembly.

SIDE PANELS. Before attaching the facings, I cut the side panels (B) to finished size; see Fig. l. Then, for holding the bottom shelf and top stretchers that are added later, there's a pair of dadoes across the inside face of each panel; see Figs. 1 and lb.

And a rabbet along the back inside edge is needed to accept a plywood back; see Fig. lb.

Now the facings can be glued to the sides. (Note: For a tip on attaching a facing to a side, see the box below.)

SHELF & DIVIDER. Next, the other two major panels, the bottom shelf (C) and center divider (D), can be cut to finished dimensions; see Fig. 2.

STRETCHERS. The shelf connects the hutch sides at the bottom. But at the top, I used a pair of stretchers; see Fig. 2. So next I cut these stretchers (E) to finished size.

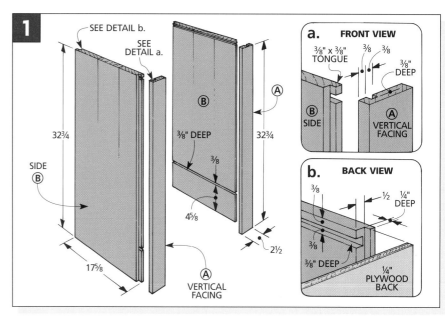

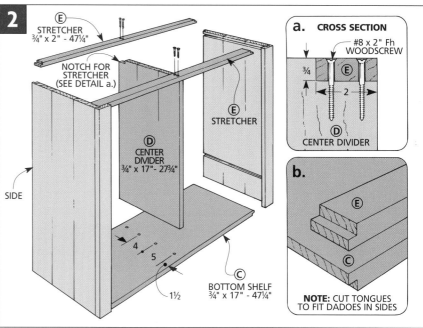

Square Corners

Most of the time when you add facing strips to a case, the case has already been built. Gluing on the facing is simply a matter of clamping the strips in place.

But I built the country hutch a bit different. I added the vertical facings to the sides *before* building the case. If the clamps aren't perfectly centered on the joint, they tend to force the facing piece out of square with the side.

To keep the pieces square, I clamped square blocks into the corner of the assembly. So the assembly is automatically pulled up square against the blocks.

Note: I cut off the inside corner of each block to allow for glue squeeze-out.

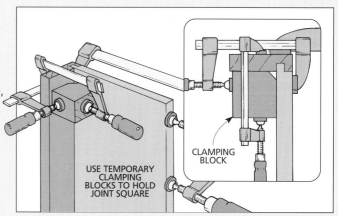

36   COUNTRY HUTCH

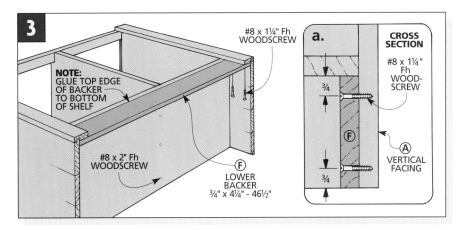

3

NOTE: GLUE TOP EDGE OF BACKER TO BOTTOM OF SHELF

#8 x 1¼" Fh WOODSCREW

#8 x 2" Fh WOODSCREW

LOWER BACKER ¾" x 4¼" - 46½"

a. CROSS SECTION

#8 x 1¼" Fh WOOD-SCREW

¾

Ⓕ

¾

VERTICAL FACING

Ⓐ

TONGUES & NOTCHES. Before the lower cabinet can be assembled, tongues must be formed on the ends of both the bottom shelf and the stretchers; see Fig. 2b. The tongues are cut to fit in the dadoes in the side panels.

Next, cut a small notch on the top corners of the center divider (D); see Figs. 2 and 2a. These permit the divider to fit between the stretchers.

ASSEMBLE UNIT. Now the lower cabinet can be assembled. I started by gluing the shelf and stretchers between the sides.

Next, install the divider with woodscrews down through the stretchers; see Fig. 2a. Also screw into the divider through the bottom shelf; see Figs. 2 and 3. Note: Position the divider so it creates two equal-size compartments inside the cabinet.

BACKER BOARD. The last structural part of the lower cabinet is a lower backer (F) that fits across the bottom of the case under the shelf; see Figs. 3 and 3a. This stiffens the shelf and makes the cabinet more rigid.

UPPER & LOWER FACINGS

There are a couple of reasons for adding facing pieces to the carcase of a cabinet. First, vertical facings give the appearance that the sides and divider are thicker. Second, the middle (horizontal) facings create the openings for the door and drawer compartments.

There's nothing tricky about cutting the facing strips, but the sequence for installing them is important. I started by gluing an upper facing (G) onto the front stretcher; see Figs. 4 and 4a.

Next, glue the lower facing (H) onto the lower backer (F); see Figs. 4 and 4b.

Note the "lip" that's created when the lower facing is attached; see Fig. 4b.

This acts as a stop for the doors installed later.

DIVIDER FACING. After the horizontal facings are in place, the divider facing (I) can be cut and glued to the edge of the divider; see Fig. 4. Then, for added strength, the top of the divider facing is secured with a pair of woodscrews; see Figs. 4 and 4a.

DRAWER BACKERS & FACINGS. By now, the base has two large, open compartments. The next step is to divide this space into drawer and shelf compartments.

To do this, I added another set of facings. But to hold the facings, I first installed a pair of middle backers (J); see Fig. 5.

Then the middle facings (K) are glued to the backers; see Figs. 5 and 5a. Note: The facings create another lip that serves as an upper stop for the doors; see Fig. 5a.

DECORATIVE COVES. After the facings were all in place there was one more step I wanted to do on the lower cabinet. I used a ¼" cove bit to rout a decorative stopped cove on the outside edge of each vertical facing piece (A); see Fig. 4. The cove starts and stops in line with the upper and lower facings. Shop Note: It's easiest to lay the cabinet on its back to rout these coves.

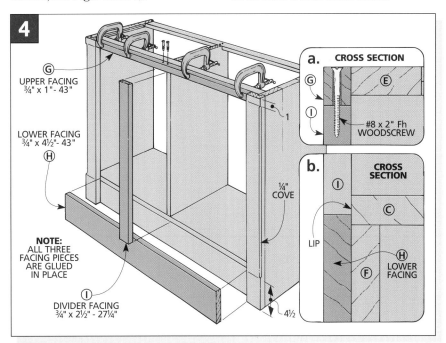

4

UPPER FACING ¾" x 1"- 43"

Ⓖ

LOWER FACING ¾" x 4½"- 43"

Ⓗ

NOTE: ALL THREE FACING PIECES ARE GLUED IN PLACE

Ⓘ

DIVIDER FACING ¾" x 2½" - 27¼"

¼" COVE

1

a. CROSS SECTION

Ⓖ   Ⓔ

Ⓘ

#8 x 2" Fh WOODSCREW

b. CROSS SECTION

Ⓘ

Ⓒ

LIP

Ⓕ   Ⓗ LOWER FACING

4½

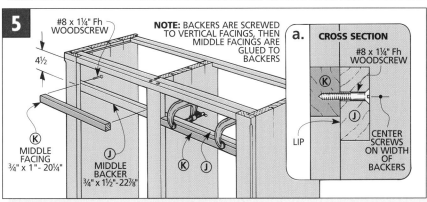

5

#8 x 1¼" Fh WOODSCREW

4½

Ⓚ

MIDDLE FACING ¾" x 1"- 20¼"

MIDDLE BACKER ¾" x 1½"-22⅞"

Ⓙ   Ⓚ Ⓙ

NOTE: BACKERS ARE SCREWED TO VERTICAL FACINGS, THEN MIDDLE FACINGS ARE GLUED TO BACKERS

a. CROSS SECTION

#8 x 1¼" Fh WOODSCREW

Ⓚ

Ⓙ

LIP

CENTER SCREWS ON WIDTH OF BACKERS

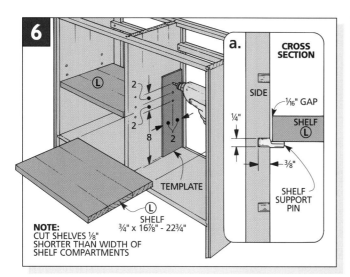

6

a. CROSS SECTION

SIDE

¹/₁₆" GAP

SHELF
Ⓛ

¹/₄"

SHELF
SUPPORT
PIN

³/₈"

TEMPLATE

SHELF
Ⓛ
³/₄" x 16⁷/₈" - 22³/₄"

NOTE:
CUT SHELVES ¹/₈"
SHORTER THAN WIDTH OF
SHELF COMPARTMENTS

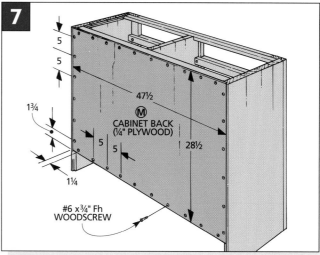

7

5
5

47½

Ⓜ
CABINET BACK
(¹/₄" PLYWOOD)

28½

1³/₄

5

5

1¼

#6 x³/₄" Fh
WOODSCREW

SHELVES & BACK

At this point, all the structural parts of the base are complete. So, before moving on to the top shelf and upper unit, I built the inside shelves and enclosed the back.

ADJUSTABLE SHELVES. I built two shelves to fit inside the lower unit — one on each side of the vertical divider. And, like the other panels, the adjustable shelves (L) are glued up from several strips of pine; see Fig. 6. For ease of installation, the shelves are cut ¹/₈" *shorter* than the width of the compartments; see Figs. 6 and 6a.

To support the shelves — and also make them adjustable — I drilled three sets of holes for each shelf; see Fig. 6.

PLYWOOD BACK. After the support holes were drilled, I enclosed the back of the unit with a piece of ¹/₄"-thick plywood; see Fig. 7. The cabinet back (M) fits in the rabbets on the back edge of the side panels.

DRAWERS, DOORS & TOP

With the shelves and back installed, I moved on to the drawers. But first there needs to be some way of attaching the drawer hardware (slides).

MOUNTING RAIL SYSTEM. Ordinarily, drawer slides are attached directly to the sides of a cabinet. But on this project that's not possible — the sides are "recessed" because of the vertical facings on the front of the cabinet sides.

So I came up with a different method of attaching the drawer slides. It's a system of mounting rails — strips of wood suspended below the stretchers; see Fig. 8.

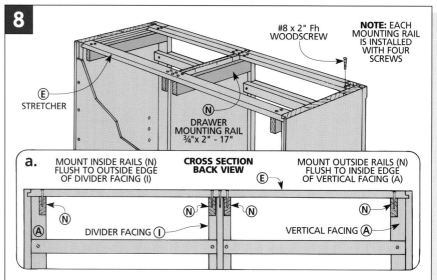

8

#8 x 2" Fh
WOODSCREW

NOTE: EACH
MOUNTING RAIL
IS INSTALLED
WITH FOUR
SCREWS

Ⓔ
STRETCHER

Ⓝ
DRAWER
MOUNTING RAIL
³/₄" x 2" - 17"

a. MOUNT INSIDE RAILS (N)
FLUSH TO OUTSIDE EDGE
OF DIVIDER FACING (I)

CROSS SECTION
BACK VIEW

MOUNT OUTSIDE RAILS (N)
FLUSH TO INSIDE EDGE
OF VERTICAL FACING (A)

Ⓔ

Ⓝ   Ⓝ   Ⓝ   Ⓝ

Ⓐ   DIVIDER FACING Ⓘ   VERTICAL FACING Ⓐ

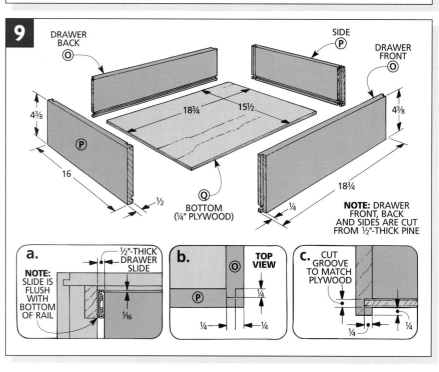

9

DRAWER
BACK
Ⓞ

SIDE
Ⓟ

DRAWER
FRONT
Ⓞ

4³/₈

18³/₄   15½

4³/₈

Ⓟ

16

½

Ⓠ

BOTTOM
(¹/₄" PLYWOOD)

¹/₄

18³/₄

NOTE: DRAWER
FRONT, BACK
AND SIDES ARE CUT
FROM ½"-THICK PINE

a.
NOTE:
SLIDE IS
FLUSH
WITH
BOTTOM
OF RAIL

½"-THICK
DRAWER
SLIDE

¹/₁₆

b.
Ⓞ

TOP
VIEW

¹/₄

Ⓟ

¹/₄   ¹/₄

c. CUT
GROOVE
TO MATCH
PLYWOOD

¹/₄   ¹/₄

After cutting the mounting rails (N) to finished dimensions, they can be installed inside the case; see Fig. 8a.

DRAWERS. Next, I moved on to the drawers. All the drawer parts, the front/backs (O) and the sides (P), are cut from $1/2$"-thick stock; see Fig. 9.

Note: There are three dimensions to consider when cutting the drawer parts. First, the drawer slides I used require $1/2$" clearance on each side; see Fig. 9a.

Second, the details of the drawer joint affect the *length* of the fronts and backs (O); see Fig. 9b.

And third, all the drawer parts are cut to *width* to allow a $1/16$" gap at the top and bottom; see Fig. 9a.

DRAWER JOINTS. After the drawer parts had been cut to finished dimensions, I cut the tongue and dado joints that hold the parts together; see Fig. 9b.

Next, to hold the drawer bottoms in place, I cut a groove along the inside face of each drawer part; see Fig. 9c. Then, the bottoms (Q) can be cut to fit in these grooves.

FALSE FRONTS. The full-extension drawer slides I used on this project need to be hidden when the drawers are closed; see Fig. 9a. That's the job of false fronts; see Fig. 10.

The false fronts (R) are cut to fit the drawer openings with an even ($1/16$") gap all around; see Fig. 10a.

Then two holes can be drilled for a pair of wood knobs; see Fig. 10a.

DRAWER SLIDES. Before the drawers can be installed, the slides need to be attached; see box below.

After the drawers are installed, the false fronts can be attached; see Fig. 10.

TOP. I completed the lower cabinet by making a top for the unit; see Fig. 11.

The top (W) is glued up from $1\frac{1}{4}$"-thick stock. After the top had been cut to finished size, I routed a decorative bullnose profile around the sides and front (but not the back); see Fig. 11a.

Finally, I screwed the top to the case through oversize ($3/16$") shank holes in the stretchers; see Fig. 11.

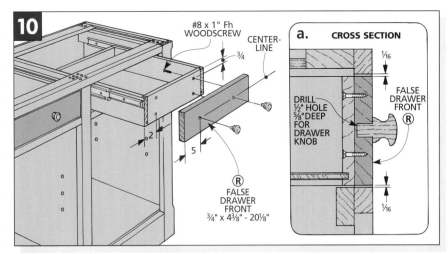

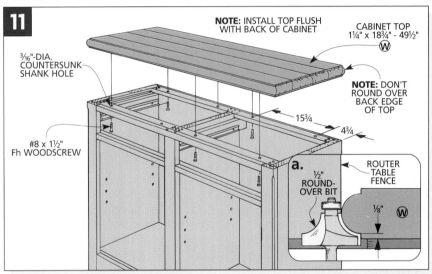

Drawer Slide Installation

I wanted to make the country hutch as traditional-looking as possible. But I wasn't going to leave out full-extension drawer slides.

Wood slides look traditional, but they also can bind under a heavy load. Full-extension slides open smooth and allow easy access to the contents at the back of the drawer.

Like any drawer hardware, these slides have to be mounted level with each other. But this can be a little trickier than with other slides. That's because the edges are typically rounded. So it's hard to line them up.

On the country hutch the mounting rails hang from the top and aren't part of the sides. So I clamped a temporary scrap piece to the bottom of the rails to create a little ledge. When the slides were set in place, they were level and perfectly flush with the bottom of the rails.

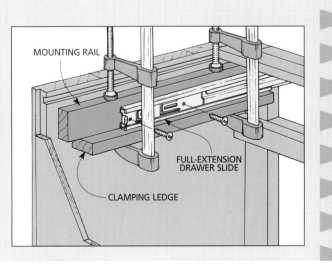

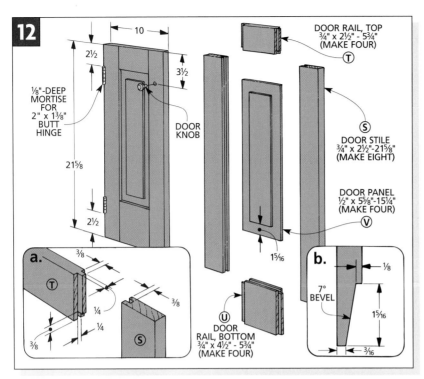

12

10

2½

3½

⅛"-DEEP MORTISE FOR 2" x 1⅜" BUTT HINGE

DOOR KNOB

21⅝

2½

DOOR RAIL, TOP
¾" x 2½" - 5¾"
(MAKE FOUR)
Ⓣ

DOOR STILE
¾" x 2½"-21⅝"
(MAKE EIGHT)
Ⓢ

DOOR PANEL
½" x 5⅝"-15¼"
(MAKE FOUR)
Ⓥ

1⁵⁄₁₆

a.
⅜
¼
Ⓣ
¼
⅜
⅜
⅜
Ⓢ

DOOR RAIL, BOTTOM
¾" x 4½" - 5¾"
(MAKE FOUR)
Ⓤ

b.
⅛
7° BEVEL
1⁵⁄₁₆
³⁄₁₆

13

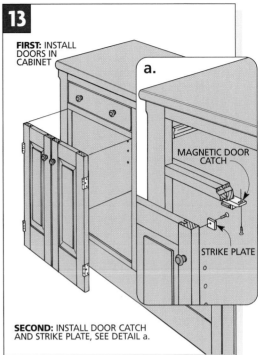

FIRST: INSTALL DOORS IN CABINET

a.

MAGNETIC DOOR CATCH

STRIKE PLATE

SECOND: INSTALL DOOR CATCH AND STRIKE PLATE, SEE DETAIL a.

DOORS

I started the doors by cutting the frame pieces. Two stiles (S) and two rails (T and U) are cut for each door; see Fig. 12. Note: The bottom rails (U) are wider than the top rails (T).

After the frame parts have been cut, grooves for the panel can be cut on the inside edges; see Fig. 12a.

Then, stub tenons are cut on the ends of the rails to fit in the grooves.

PANELS. The door panels (V) are made from ½"-thick pine. To allow for expansion and contraction, they should be cut ⅛" *smaller* than the distance between the grooves; see Fig. 12.

After the panels have been cut to size, I used the table saw to cut a bevel all around the front face; see box below.

Now, all the doors can be assembled with glue in the corner joints *only*, not around the panel. It must be free to "float" when it expands and contracts.

HINGES & KNOBS. Before the doors can be installed, ⅛"-deep mortises are cut for the hinges; see Fig. 12.

After installing the hinges, I drilled a ⅝"-deep hole on the front for the door knob (the same as the drawers); see Fig. 12. Then the knobs can be glued in.

Finally, the doors can be installed and adjusted for an equal ¹⁄₁₆" gap around and between them.

DOOR CATCHES. Now the catch and strike plate can be installed; see Fig. 13.

Cutting Raised Panels Safely

I never feel safe standing a narrow piece on edge and running it unsupported through the saw when cut-ting a raised panel. It isn't very stable, and it's hard to hold the piece tight against the fence and keep your fin-gers away from the blade.

If you don't want to take the time to build a jig, one quick solution is to screw a tall auxiliary fence to the rip fence and clamp a couple of handscrew clamps to the panel; see drawing at left. The handscrews ride along the top of the fence and provide added support.

Once you've cut the bevel, there are usually some saw marks to be sanded off. To remove these, I made a sanding block with a beveled edge to square up the angled shoulder; see below.

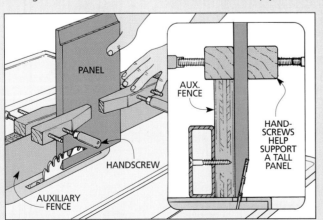

PANEL

AUXILIARY FENCE

HANDSCREW

AUX. FENCE

HAND-SCREWS HELP SUPPORT A TALL PANEL

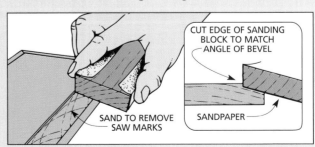

SAND TO REMOVE SAW MARKS

CUT EDGE OF SANDING BLOCK TO MATCH ANGLE OF BEVEL

SANDPAPER

UPPER CABINET

At this point the lower cabinet is complete. By adding an upper cabinet, the project becomes a hutch.

FACINGS & SIDES. The upper cabinet is built much like the lower one. First, facings (X) are glued to the sides (Y); see Fig. 14. Then a stopped cove is routed on the front edges.

The main difference between the two units is at the back. Instead of a rabbet, there's a groove; see Fig. 14b.

BACK RAILS. Back slats enclose the back of the upper unit; see Figs. 15 and 18. These are held in place by a pair of rails. Note: The upper rail (Z) is narrower than the lower rail (AA).

After cutting the rails to size, cut rabbets to form a short offset tenon on the end of each rail; see Fig. 16. This fits in the groove in the sides.

The other joinery on the rails is a simple rabbet that accepts the back slats; see Figs. 17 and 19a (on page 42).

COVES. Finally, I routed a ¼" stopped cove on each rail; see Fig. 15.

BACK SLATS. The back is enclosed with thirteen back slats. All the slats are cut to the same length from ¾"-thick pine; see Fig. 15. The only thing that's a bit unusual here is the width of the slats.

The two outside slats (BB) are wider than the eleven inside slats (CC). That's because the tongues on the outside slats are hidden.

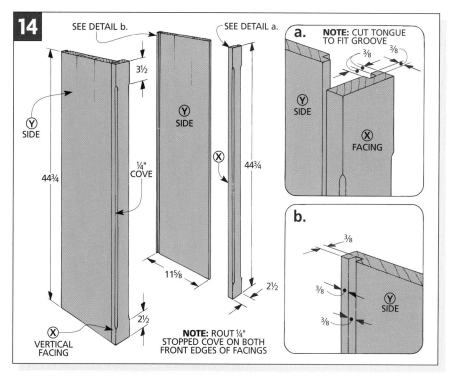

After cutting the slats to finished dimensions, a centered groove for a spline is cut on *both* edges of the inside slats (CC); see Figs. 18 and 18a.

Then, an identical groove is cut on just the *inside* edge of the outside slats (BB). Finally, a rabbet is cut on the *outside* edge of the outside slats; see Figs. 18 and 18a.

CHAMFERS. Before the slats were installed, I routed decorative chamfers

on both edges of the inside slats, but only on one edge of the outside slats; see Fig. 18a.

SPLINES. Now that the slats are cut there needs to be a way to keep them all aligned. That's the job of the splines; see Fig. 18.

The twelve splines (DD) are ripped from ¾"-thick pine to width (¼") so they fit in the grooves in each of the slats; see Fig. 18a.

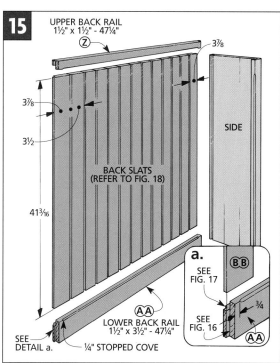

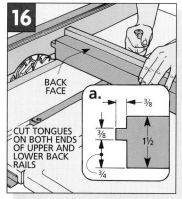

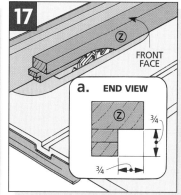

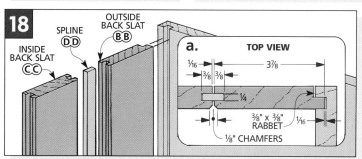

UPPER CABINET ASSEMBLY

Now the upper unit can be assembled. To do this, I found it easiest to first attach the slats between the top and bottom rails. Don't forget to install a spline (without any glue) between each of the slats.

I started by screwing the outside slats to the rails so the edge of each outside slat aligns with the end of the tenon on the rails.

Then screw down the inside slats (again, don't use any glue) so there's a consistent-size ($^1/_{16}$") gap between all of the slats. This will allow room for the wood to expand and contract with changes in humidity.

With the back slats and rails assembled as a unit, the sides of the cabinet can be glued on; see Fig. 19.

VALANCE & TOP

Now the side can be connected across the front by a strip called a valance.

VALANCE. The valance (EE) starts out as a long strip cut to fit between the vertical facings, see Fig. 20. Note: When measuring for the valance, the back unit must be square (90°) to the sides of the cabinet.

To lay out the arch shape, first make pencil marks to indicate the ends of the arc; see Fig. 21. Then make a mark to indicate the top of the arc. Now, connect the marks using a thin stick as a guide for the pencil. (Nails hold the stick while the curve is drawn.)

Next, the arched profile can be cut on the band saw or sabre saw. Then sand the arch smooth and rout a decorative $^1/_4$" stopped cove along the bottom edge; see Fig. 21a.

SCREW BLOCKS. There's a simple way to attach the valance between the vertical facings. It involves a pair of $^1/_2$"-thick screw blocks (FF) that are glued and screwed to the back of the facings. Then the valance is screwed to the blocks; see Figs. 20 and 20a.

TOP. The top (GG) of the upper unit is just like the top of the lower unit. It's glued up from $1^1/_4$"-thick stock then cut to size; see Fig. 22. Note: The edges of this top are left square (no profile).

The top can now be screwed to the sides (Y), back rail, and valance; see Figs. 22 and 22a. Note: There should be an equal (1") overhang on the sides and front but no overhang at the back.

MOLDING. The edges of the top aren't routed, but there is a decorative detail. It's a strip of molding (HH) attached below the top with 4d finish nails; see Figs. 22 and 22a. After setting the nails, fill the holes with putty.

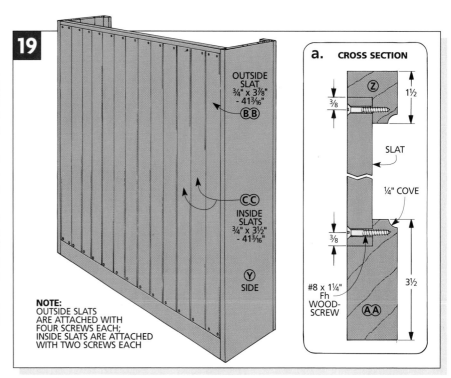

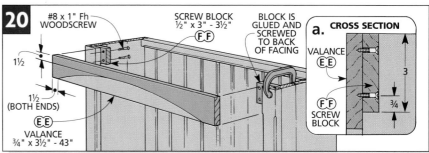

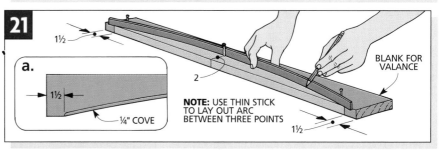

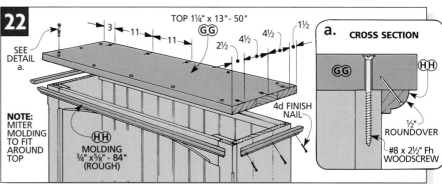

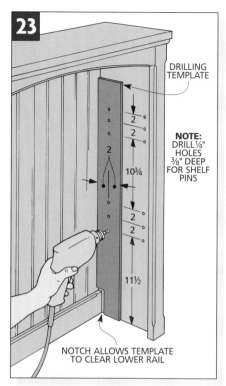

23

DRILLING TEMPLATE

2
2
2
10¾
2
2
11½

NOTE: DRILL ¼" HOLES ⅜" DEEP FOR SHELF PINS

NOTCH ALLOWS TEMPLATE TO CLEAR LOWER RAIL

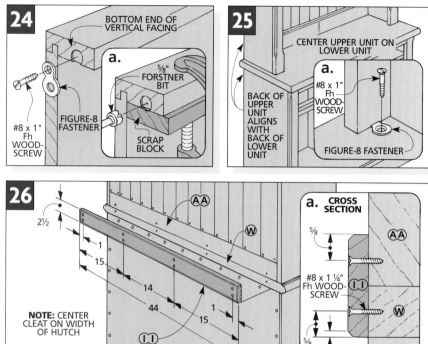

24

BOTTOM END OF VERTICAL FACING

a.

⅝" FORSTNER BIT

#8 x 1" Fh WOOD-SCREW

FIGURE-8 FASTENER

SCRAP BLOCK

25

CENTER UPPER UNIT ON LOWER UNIT

a.

#8 x 1" Fh WOOD-SCREW

BACK OF UPPER UNIT ALIGNS WITH BACK OF LOWER UNIT

FIGURE-8 FASTENER

26

2½
1
15
14
44
1
15

NOTE: CENTER CLEAT ON WIDTH OF HUTCH

CONNECTING CLEAT

a. CROSS SECTION

⅝

#8 x 1¼" Fh WOOD-SCREW

⅝

⅛" CHAMFER

TOP SHELVES

The upper half of the hutch is almost ready to be placed on the lower half, but there's one thing to do first.

SHELF HOLES. I planned to add two shelves to the upper unit. And I wanted each shelf to be adjustable. So before attaching the upper unit to the lower case, I drilled twelve holes in each side for shelf support pins; see Fig. 23.

Shop Note: I used the same trick used for the shelf support pins on the lower unit — a piece of hardboard as a template for drilling the holes; see Fig. 23. Always align the template flush with the bottom edge of the cabinet so the holes will line up.

FIGURE-8 FASTENERS. Now the upper unit can be attached to the lower unit. To do this, first install a pair of "Figure-8" fasteners on the bottom end of each vertical facing (X); see Fig. 24.

In order for the upper unit to pull tight to the lower unit, the fasteners must be recessed into the facings. This is done by drilling a shallow hole on the bottom of each facing; see Fig. 24a.

Shop Tip: Each hole should be drilled slightly off center of the facing. To keep the drill bit from wandering as I drilled, I used a piece of scrap clamped to the facing as a guide for the drill bit; see Fig. 24a.

After the fasteners have been screwed to the facings, the upper unit can be attached to the lower unit; see Figs. 25 and 25a.

CONNECTING CLEAT. The method I used to attach the top unit to the bottom unit at the back is fairly straightforward. It's a cleat that's screwed across both units; see Fig. 26.

After cutting the connecting cleat (II) to finished size, I chamfered the edges; see Fig. 26a. Then the cleat can be screwed to the back of the upper and lower units.

SHELVES. The last part of this project is one of the easiest — building two shelves (JJ) to fit inside the upper unit; see Fig. 27.

Note: Because these shelves have a longer span than the shelves in the lower unit, they're made from 1¼"-thick pine.

After the shelves have been cut to fit inside the top unit, I next used a cove bit to rout a decorative edge along the front of each shelf; see Fig. 27b. This ties the shelves in with the rest of the project.

Finally, I routed a pair of grooves along the top of each shelf to act as plate holders. For this, I switched to a ⅜" core box bit in the router table; see Figs. 27 and 27a. The router table fence acts as a guide for routing the plate grooves — two different setups are all that are needed. ■

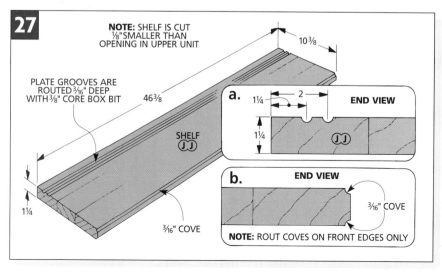

27

NOTE: SHELF IS CUT ⅛" SMALLER THAN OPENING IN UPPER UNIT

10⅜

PLATE GROOVES ARE ROUTED 3⁄16" DEEP WITH ⅜" CORE BOX BIT

46⅜

SHELF (JJ)

1¼

3⁄16" COVE

a.
1¼
2
END VIEW
1¼
(JJ)

b.
END VIEW
3⁄16" COVE
NOTE: ROUT COVES ON FRONT EDGES ONLY

Some people think of pine as a "utility wood." You know, shelves in the garage. But I also like to build furniture from pine, such as the country hutch on page 33 and pie safe on page 23.

BUYING PINE

Since pine and other softwoods are commonly used in building construction, the dimensions are fairly standard.

THICKNESS. If you ask for "1 by" material (such as 1x6 or 1x8) it should measure $3/4$" thick; see the chart. The stock was sawed off the log at 1", but measured $3/4$" after drying and planing.

WIDTH. The widths of softwood are also standard. A 1x6 should actually measure $5^{1}/_{2}$" wide if you buy it in New York or San Diego.

If the project you're building calls for $3^{3}/_{8}$"-wide pieces, you could use 1x4's (actually $3^{1}/_{2}$"-wide) and trim off $1/_{8}$".

But from my experience, 1x4's are not usually straight, and if there is any warp, they won't be wide enough to cut straight. By using 1x8's ($7^{1}/_{4}$"-wide), you can rip two pieces and have extra to work with.

GRADES. One myth about building with pine is that it's a lot less expensive than hardwood. But this isn't always the case. Using clear C select pine can cost almost as much as building out of oak. If you use No. 2 common pine, the cost is cut nearly in half. But the boards will more than likely be warped and covered with knots and defects.

So how can you build a project at a reasonable cost and still have it look good? The trick is going through the stack of No. 2 common pine at the lumberyard and picking out the straightest, clearest pieces. Then buy more than you need (usually about 20% more), and cut out the worst knots and defects. It will still cost less than the C select pine.

BUY DRY WOOD. One more thing. Only buy pine that's been kiln-dried and find a retailer that stores the pine inside.

If you can't find pine that's been stored indoors, let it set in your shop for at least a couple of weeks. Then, if warping occurs because of a change in humidity, you can cut or plane the workpieces straight before you begin to work on your project.

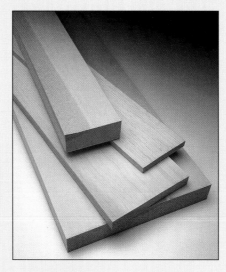

THICKNESS STANDARDS FOR PINE	
NOMINAL	ACTUAL*
1" (ONE BY)	$3/_{4}$"
2" (TWO BY)	$1^{1}/_{2}$"
4" (FOUR BY)	$3^{1}/_{2}$"
*Measured thickness after drying and surfacing.	

WIDTH STANDARDS FOR PINE	
NOMINAL	ACTUAL*
2"	$1^{1}/_{2}$"
4"	$3^{1}/_{2}$"
6"	$5^{1}/_{2}$"
8"	$7^{1}/_{4}$"
10"	$9^{1}/_{4}$"
12"	$11^{1}/_{4}$"
*Measured width after ripping edges straight.	

HANDLING

One problem with pine is that it dents easily — it doesn't take much to scratch and break the fibers. So to make my shop "pine friendly," I first give it a good cleaning. I put away tools I'm not using and sweep off the bench. Chips and dried glue that I don't normally bother with get cleaned up.

Also, on a big project like the country hutch, I'll use a sheet of plywood for a "furniture sled." Then the project sits on the plywood instead of the concrete floor.

But you can't avoid scratches and dents completely. They're inevitable — but not fatal. Most scratches can be sanded out quickly. And most dents can be removed too. I use a hot iron and a damp cloth. Place the damp cloth on the dent and heat it with the iron. The dents will soak up moisture and disappear.

TECHNIQUE

Just as important as handling pine is how you work it. The first thing I do is make sure the table saw blade is sharp. A dull blade tears the soft fibers instead of cutting them clean.

Also keep an eye on pitch buildup on the blade. It creates more resistance during the cut and the wood will burn.

DRILLING. Boring holes in pine can also be tricky. When I used a new brad point bit on the country hutch, it took chunks out of the wood at the start. I found it helped to first run the drill by hand in reverse. That way the points on the bit scribe the outside diameter of the hole slicing the wood fibers.

GLUING & SANDING

Just as the fibers in pine get torn when cutting and drilling, you can also tear them out when removing dried glue — especially if you try to scrape it off.

So first I make sure not to use too much glue on the joints. And any excess glue is scraped off *just* before it dries completely. Removing the excess now prevents tearing the fibers later.

SANDING. Sanding pine has its own special challenges. Normally I'd use a finish sander to complete a project. But on pine it leaves nearly invisible swirl marks — until it's stained. So I finish sand my projects by hand with a sanding block. Pine is made up of both soft and hard fibers (early and late wood). When you sand without a block, you remove more of the soft earlywood fibers. What you end up with is a wavy surface instead of a smooth flat one.

STAINING

When staining pine, there are a couple of things to keep in mind that will give you a better-looking project.

First, pine doesn't absorb stain evenly so you get dark blotches on the wood. Try using a stain controller or "conditioner" first. It evens out the amount of stain that soaks in.

Second, pick lighter colored stains if possible. They don't highlight missed dents, broken fibers, or swirl marks as much as dark colors.

MODULAR CABINETS

This project was designed with flexibility in mind. Standardized units can be mixed and matched to create your own custom cabinets.

When designing these cabinets, I had two goals in mind. I wanted them to be flexible so they could be customized. And portable so they could be moved easily.

For flexibility, I designed modular cabinets. There's a standard cabinet that can stand alone, or you can stack cabinets on top of each other and place them side-by-side.

Plus, there are several options for each unit. They can be left open or have glass or wood paneled doors. And a lower cabinet can be made deeper than a standard cabinet so it stands out a little more from the wall.

PORTABILITY. I mentioned another goal in designing these cabinets: portability. To save my back (I'm not as young as I used to be), I built these cab-

inets using knock-down hardware. It's no more work. In fact, knock-down hardware makes the joinery downright easy. And once all of the parts are built in your shop, it's simple to reassemble it in any room in the house.

MATERIALS AND FINISH. I built the cabinets from solid cherry and cherry plywood. And I finished them with General Finishes' Royal Finish.

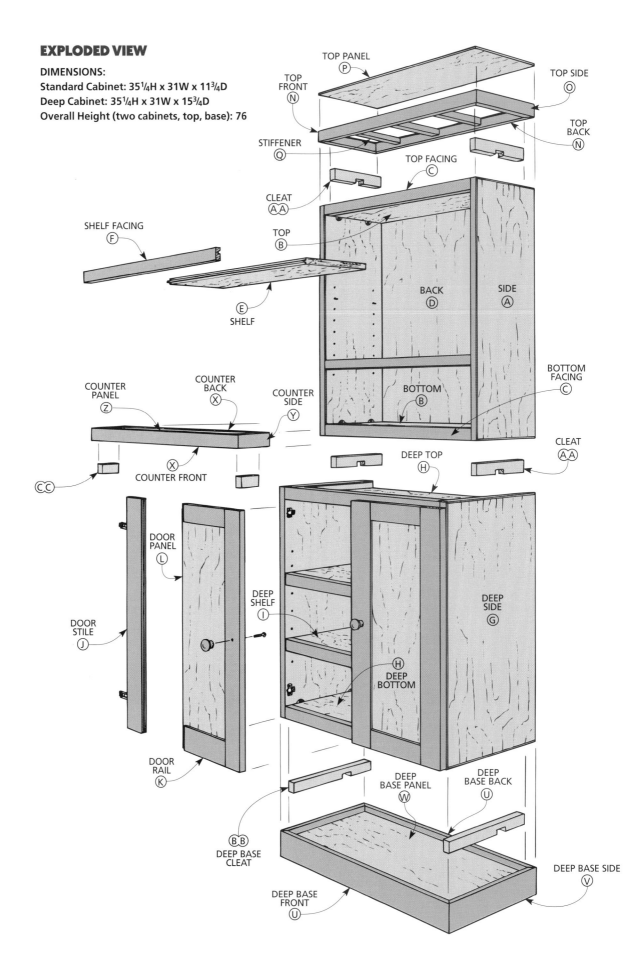

EXPLODED VIEW

DIMENSIONS:

Standard Cabinet: 35¼H x 31W x 11¾D

Deep Cabinet: 35¼H x 31W x 15¾D

Overall Height (two cabinets, top, base): 76

TOP PANEL
P

TOP FRONT
N

TOP SIDE
O

TOP BACK
N

STIFFENER
Q

TOP FACING
C

CLEAT
AA

SHELF FACING
F

TOP
B

SHELF
E

BACK
D

SIDE
A

COUNTER PANEL
Z

COUNTER BACK
X

COUNTER SIDE
Y

BOTTOM
B

BOTTOM FACING
C

CLEAT
AA

DEEP TOP
H

COUNTER FRONT
X

CC

DOOR PANEL
L

DEEP SHELF
I

DEEP SIDE
G

DOOR STILE
J

DEEP BOTTOM
H

DOOR RAIL
K

DEEP BASE PANEL
W

DEEP BASE BACK
U

BB
DEEP BASE CLEAT

DEEP BASE SIDE
V

DEEP BASE FRONT
U

MATERIALS LIST

STANDARD CABINET
A Sides (2) ¾ ply - 11¾ x 35¼
B Top/Btm. (2) ¾ ply - 11¼ x 29½
C Top/Btm Facings (2) ¾ x 1½ - 29½
D Back (1) ¼ ply - 30 x 32¾
E Shelves (2) ¾ ply - 10¾ x 29⅜
F Shelf Facings (2) ¾ x 1½ - 29⅜

DEEP CABINET*
G Dp. Sides (2) ¾ ply - 15¾ x 35¼
H Dp. Top/Btm. (2) ¾ ply - 15¼ x 29½
I Dp. Shelves (2) ¾ ply - 14¾ x 29⅜

DOORS
J Stiles (4) ¾ x 2½ - 33¾
K Rails (4) ¾ x 2½ - 10⅞
L Panels (2) ¼ ply - 10¾ x 29⅛
M Glass Stops ¼ x ⅜ - 16 lineal ft.

TOP
N Front/Back (2) ¾ x 1½ - 31
O Sides (2) ¾ x 1½ - 11¾
P Panel (1) ¼ ply - 11 x 30¼
Q Stiffeners (3) ¾ x ¾ - 10¼

STANDARD BASE
R Front/Back (2) ¾ x 4 - 31
S Sides (2) ¾ x 4 - 11¾
T Panel (1) ¼ ply - 11 x 30¼

DEEP BASE
U Dp. Front/Back (2) ¾ x 4 - 31
V Dp. Sides (2) ¾ x 4 - 15¾
W Dp. Panel (1) ¼ ply - 15 x 30¼

COUNTER
X Front/Back (2) ¾ x 1½ - 31
Y Sides (2) ¾ x 1½ - 4
Z Panel (1) ¼ ply - 3¼ x 30¼

CLEATS
AA Cleats (4) ¾ ply - 1½ x 10¼
BB Dp. Cleats (2) ¾ ply - 1½ x 14¼
CC Counter Cleats (2) ¾ ply - 1½ x 2½

*Also Needed: Facings (C & F) and Back (D)

HARDWARE SUPPLIES
#8 x 1¼" Fh Woodscrews
Blum Knock-down Fittings
125° Overlay Hinges
Connector Bolts (optional)
Spoon-style Shelf Supports
1⅛"-dia. Wood Knobs
⅛"-thick Glass (optional) with ½" brads

Note: The quantity of supplies will vary depending on the number of cabinets built.

CUTTING DIAGRAM

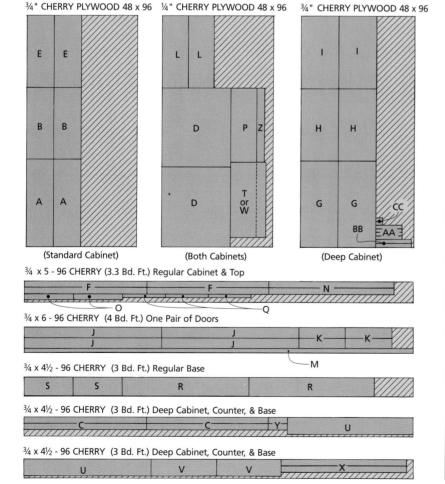

¾" CHERRY PLYWOOD 48 x 96 — (Standard Cabinet)
¼" CHERRY PLYWOOD 48 x 96 — (Both Cabinets)
¾" CHERRY PLYWOOD 48 x 96 — (Deep Cabinet)

¾ x 5 - 96 CHERRY (3.3 Bd. Ft.) Regular Cabinet & Top
¾ x 6 - 96 CHERRY (4 Bd. Ft.) One Pair of Doors
¾ x 4½ - 96 CHERRY (3 Bd. Ft.) Regular Base
¾ x 4½ - 96 CHERRY (3 Bd. Ft.) Deep Cabinet, Counter, & Base
¾ x 4½ - 96 CHERRY (3 Bd. Ft.) Deep Cabinet, Counter, & Base

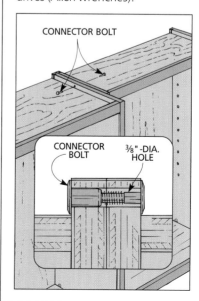

Connecting the Cabinets

Each modular cabinet is built separately, but they can be stacked on top of each other and lined up side-by-side; see photo above.

When they're stacked *on top* of each other, cleats are attached to the upper unit that nest into the top of the lower unit; see Exploded View. Gravity and a friction fit hold them together.

To connect two units *side-by-side,* I used connector bolts. A connector bolt consists of a bolt and a threaded cap nut. I fit them in holes drilled through the lips that run around the top of each cabinet; see drawing below.

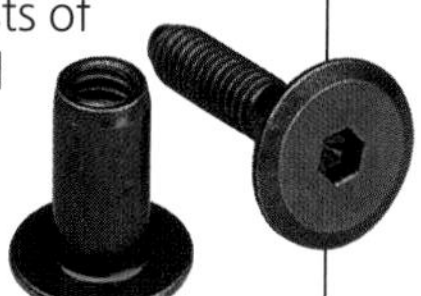

Since the hole in the cabinet is a little larger than the bolt, the cabinets can be adjusted to align across the front. Once they align, the bolt can be tightened with a pair of hex drives (Allen wrenches).

CONNECTOR BOLT

CONNECTOR BOLT

⅜"-DIA. HOLE

CABINETS

To see just how easy these cabinets are to build, take a look at a single standard cabinet; see Fig. 1.

Each standard cabinet is made up of a pair of sides, top, bottom, and ¼" plywood back. The sides are identical. So are the top and bottom; one is simply flipped "upside down;" see Fig. 1b.

You can also build deep cabinets. The only difference is that the sides, top, and bottom are 4" deeper than on the standard cabinet; see Fig. 1a.

SIDES. To build the cabinets, I started by cutting the sides (A) to size from ¾"-thick plywood. Then I covered the exposed plywood edges of the side panels — top, bottom, and front — with veneer. Adding the edging not only hides the plywood, it also helps protect the face veneer from chipping.

Note: You can buy veneer edging, but the color may not match your plywood. For a perfect match, I made my own veneer edging from some leftover pieces of plywood; see page 53.

TOP & BOTTOM. With the side edges veneered, work can begin on the top and bottom panels. I cut the top and bottom (B) to length, but cut them a little wide at first (11½"). This way they can be cut to match the width of the sides after the facing (C) is added later.

Unlike the side panels, the top and bottom panels have edging applied to their *front* edges only. And this time, I used ¾"-thick hardwood facing (C) that I ripped 1½" wide; see Fig. 1b. This facing does more than just hide the plywood; it also adds strength to the panels and prevents them from sagging.

To help align the facing flush with the panel, I cut a ¼" x ¼" groove in the facing and a mating tongue on the panel; see Figs. 2 and 2a. Then I glued them together.

After the glue is dry, rip the top and bottom panels to width. The important

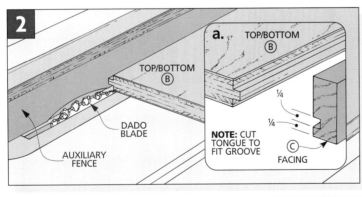

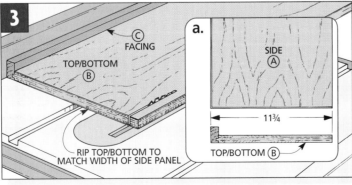

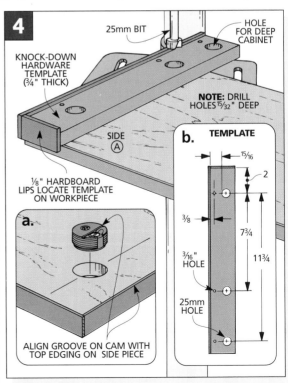

thing is that they match the width of the edged side panels; see Figs. 3 and 3a. (The standard cabinets are 11¾". The deep ones are 15¾"; see Fig. 1a.)

GROOVE FOR BACK. The next step is to cut a groove on all the pieces to hold the back; see Figs. 1 and 1b. This groove is ¼" deep and just wide enough to hold a ¼" plywood panel.

KNOCK-DOWN HARDWARE. Now the side, top, and bottom panels are ready for the knock-down fasteners. There are two main parts to these fasteners: a metal cam housed in a piece of plastic about the size of a quarter, and a pin that looks like an overgrown screw; refer to Fig. 6 and 6a. (Note: These fasteners and the drill bits needed to install them are available from some of the sources listed on page 95.)

This hardware simply requires drilling 25mm holes in the side panels for the cams (see Fig. 4) and ³⁄₁₆" holes in the top and bottom panels for the pins; see Fig. 5. To make this as easy and accurate as possible, I made a drilling template; see Fig. 4b. (Note: The template has three sets of holes. This way, it will work with the deep cabinets as well as the standard ones.)

Once the holes are drilled, tap the cams in with a rubber mallet and screw the pins in with a screwdriver.

BACK. After the hardware is installed, the next step is to dry assemble the cabinet to measure for the back panel; see Fig. 6. (It fits in the grooves you cut earlier; see Fig. 6b.) After the back (D) is cut to size, the cabinet is ready to be assembled. But you won't need any glue or clamps. Because of the knock-down hardware, the cabinet goes together with just a Phillips screwdriver; see Fig. 6a.

SHELVES. Finally, I added the shelves. These shelves rest on spoon-style supports; see Fig. 7b. So first, I drilled a series of holes to accept the supports. And again I used a shop-made template to make this process faster and more accurate than laying out each hole by hand; see Fig. 7a and 7b.

The shelves (E) and shelf facing (F) are built the same way as the top and bottom panels — tongue and groove joinery. But there are a couple differences. They don't have any grooves at the back, and they're sized to fit inside the cabinet. In my case, the finished size of a standard cabinet shelf (with facing) was 11¼"-wide and 29⅜"-long.

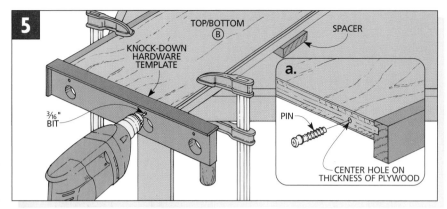

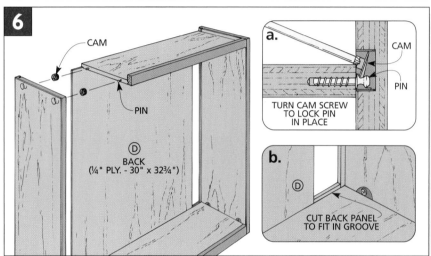

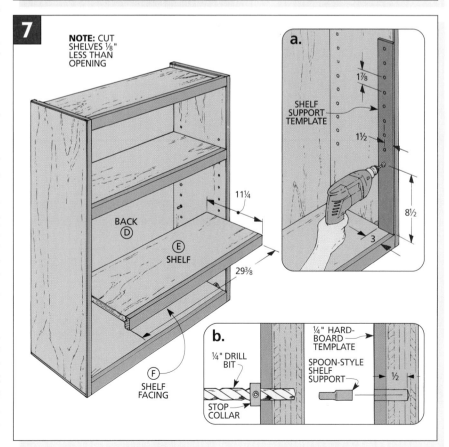

DOORS

Like the cabinets, I kept the doors simple. Just a hardwood frame around a panel, all held together with stub tenon and groove joints. And you can choose either $\frac{1}{8}$"-thick glass or $\frac{1}{4}$" plywood for the panels.

Even hanging the doors is easy. I used European-style hinges that snap on and off. And they're adjustable, so after the doors are installed, you can fine-tune the fit, if needed. (For more on these hinges; see pages 54 and 55.)

STILES & RAILS. To build the doors, I began by making the stiles (J) and rails (K) from $\frac{3}{4}$"-thick stock; see Fig. 8. The width of all these pieces is $2\frac{1}{2}$". But the stiles and rails are different lengths. To find the lengths, you need to determine the overall size of the doors.

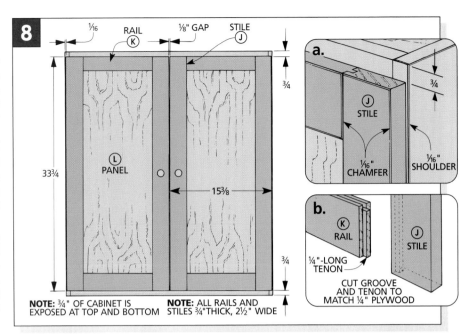

8

$\frac{1}{16}$ RAIL (K) $\frac{1}{8}$" GAP STILE (J)

$\frac{3}{4}$

$33\frac{3}{4}$ PANEL (L)

$15\frac{3}{8}$

$\frac{3}{4}$

NOTE: $\frac{3}{4}$" OF CABINET IS EXPOSED AT TOP AND BOTTOM

NOTE: ALL RAILS AND STILES $\frac{3}{4}$"THICK, $2\frac{1}{2}$" WIDE

a.

STILE (J) $\frac{3}{4}$

$\frac{1}{16}$" CHAMFER $\frac{1}{16}$" SHOULDER

b.

RAIL (K) STILE (J)

$\frac{1}{4}$"-LONG TENON

CUT GROOVE AND TENON TO MATCH $\frac{1}{4}$" PLYWOOD

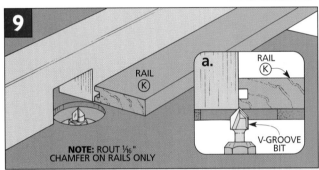

9

RAIL (K)

a. RAIL (K)

V-GROOVE BIT

NOTE: ROUT $\frac{1}{16}$" CHAMFER ON RAILS ONLY

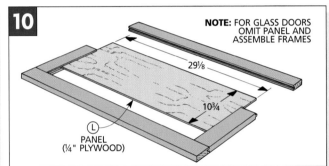

10

NOTE: FOR GLASS DOORS OMIT PANEL AND ASSEMBLE FRAMES

$29\frac{1}{8}$

$10\frac{3}{4}$

PANEL (L) ($\frac{1}{4}$" PLYWOOD)

The stiles are cut $1\frac{1}{2}$" shorter than the height of the cabinets; see Fig. 8. (Mine were $33\frac{3}{4}$" long.) That's because the doors lay over the cabinets, leaving $\frac{3}{4}$" exposed at the top and bottom.

Arriving at the length of the rails takes a little more work. What you want to end up with are two doors with $\frac{1}{16}$" of the cabinet exposed on both edges and a $\frac{1}{8}$" gap between the doors. Plus, you have to allow for the width of the stiles and the $\frac{1}{4}$"-long tenons on both ends of the rails. (My rails were $10\frac{7}{8}$" long.)

STUB TENON & GROOVE. Now to join the stiles and rails, first cut a groove on the inside edge of all the pieces; see Fig. 8b. Then cut stub tenons on the rails to fit in the grooves.

CHAMFER. Before assembling the doors, I decided to add a chamfer around the inside edge of the frame. This was a two–step procedure.

First, I used a V-groove bit to rout a chamfer on the inside edge of the rails only; see Fig. 9. Later, *after* the frame was glued up, I routed the chamfer on the stiles; refer to Fig. 11.

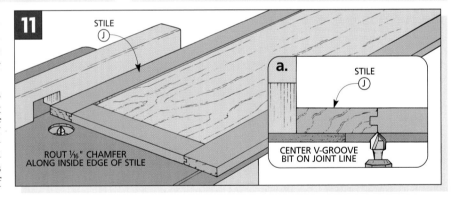

11

STILE (J)

a. STILE (J)

ROUT $\frac{1}{16}$" CHAMFER ALONG INSIDE EDGE OF STILE

CENTER V-GROOVE BIT ON JOINT LINE

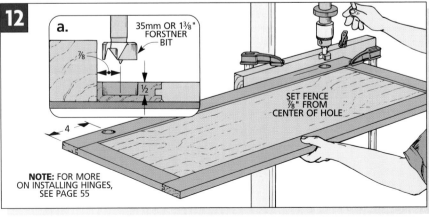

12

a. 35mm OR $1\frac{3}{8}$" FORSTNER BIT

$\frac{7}{8}$ $\frac{1}{2}$

4

SET FENCE $\frac{7}{8}$" FROM CENTER OF HOLE

NOTE: FOR MORE ON INSTALLING HINGES, SEE PAGE 55

Glass Panels

Even though you don't want to install the glass in the doors before the finish is applied, you can still get everything ready. After the chamfer has been completed on the outside of a door, a rabbet can be routed on the inside face; see left drawing. To hold the ⅛"-thick glass, I cut some thin strips to act as stops (M); see right drawing.

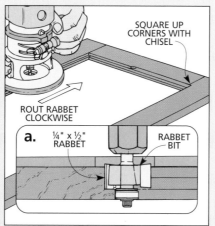

ROUT RABBET: First, rout a ¼" rabbet ½" deep around the inside of the door frame. Then square up the corners with a chisel.

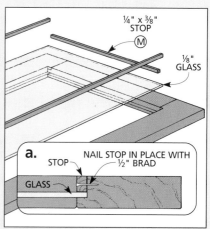

CUT STOPS: Next cut ¼" x ⅜" stops to hold the ⅛"-thick glass panel. Be sure to predrill pilot holes before tacking the stops in place.

ASSEMBLY. Next, the plywood panels (L) can be cut to fit inside the frames, and the doors can be assembled; see Fig. 10.

With the doors glued up, the chamfers can now be completed; see Fig. 11. This chamfer runs the full length of the stile. Simply set the router fence so the bit follows the joint line; see Fig. 11a. Then make a pass along the full length of each stile.

When that's done, rout another small chamfer (¹/₁₆") on the outside edge of each door.

GLASS DOORS. If you're adding glass to some of the doors, now's the time to rout the rabbet and make the stops (M) that hold the glass; see the box above. Note: It's a good idea to actually install the glass *after* the finish is applied to the door frame and stops.

MOUNTING THE DOORS. Now the doors can be mounted. This is easy with European-style hinges. The hinge goes in a hole on the door; see Fig. 12. And the mounting plate fits inside the cabinet; see Fig. 13. (Again, for more on these hinges; see pages 54 and 55.)

The really nice thing about these hinges is that they come apart so each half can be mounted separately; see Fig. 13. Once they're in place, the hinges just snap together; see Fig. 14.

With the doors mounted, the last step is to add a wood knob centered on the stiles; see Fig. 15.

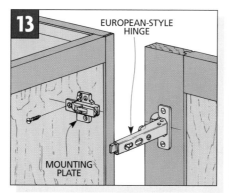

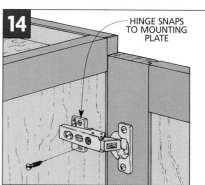

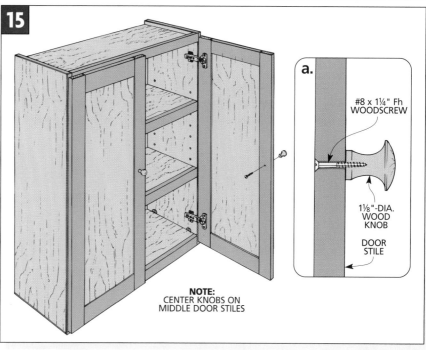

TOP, COUNTER, & BASE

Once all the individual modules were complete, I began to put everything together. This required more parts.

To finish off the standard cabinets, I added a framed top panel; see Figs. 16 and Fig. 16a. There's also a counter to cover the exposed section of the deeper cabinet (Fig. 16b), and a base frame to raise the cabinet off the floor (Fig. 16c.)

These parts are all similar. They're hardwood frames strengthened with plywood panels and built to match the width and depth of the cabinets.

TOP. I started with the top. First, the $3/4$"-thick pieces (parts N and O) are ripped $1^1/2$"-wide (tall). Then they're mitered to length so the assembled frame will match the top of the cabinet.

To add stability to the frame, all the pieces are rabbeted to hold a $1/4$" plywood panel (P); see Fig. 16a.

After the frame and panel were assembled, I glued three stiffeners (Q) underneath. This adds extra support in case anything heavy is set on the top.

And to "hide" the line between the top frame and the cabinet below, I cut a small rabbet ($1/8$" x $1/8$") around the bottom edge on the front and sides.

COUNTER. The counter is like a narrow top unit but without the stiffeners; see Fig. 16b. (You only need it if you build a deep lower cabinet.) Its purpose is to cover the exposed opening on top of the deep cabinet. The top surface of the counter should be flush with the inside of the cabinet above.

BASE. Finally, I added a base underneath each lower cabinet; see Fig. 16c. It's a little different from the top unit.

First, the frame of the base is taller. Another difference is where the plywood panel is located. Instead of being flush with the top, the panel is held in a groove that's cut $3/4$" down from the top. This provides room for cleats that will align the cabinet and base later. Also, like the counter, there's no need for stiffeners underneath the plywood.

FINAL ASSEMBLY. After the top, counter, and base frames are complete, it's time to put the whole thing together.

To hold two cabinets together side-to-side, I used connector bolts; refer to page 47. (They're not needed if you're only building one set of cabinets.)

To stack the cabinets, I added cleats (AA, BB) to keep them aligned; see Fig. 16. The plywood cleats are $1^1/2$"-wide

with a notch cut in them to fit around the head of the connector bolts.

The cleats are screwed beneath the top frame and each of the cabinets; see Figs. 16a and c. Then the cleats fit into the cabinet (or base) below.

Also glue two small cleats (CC) underneath the counter; see Fig. 16b. ∎

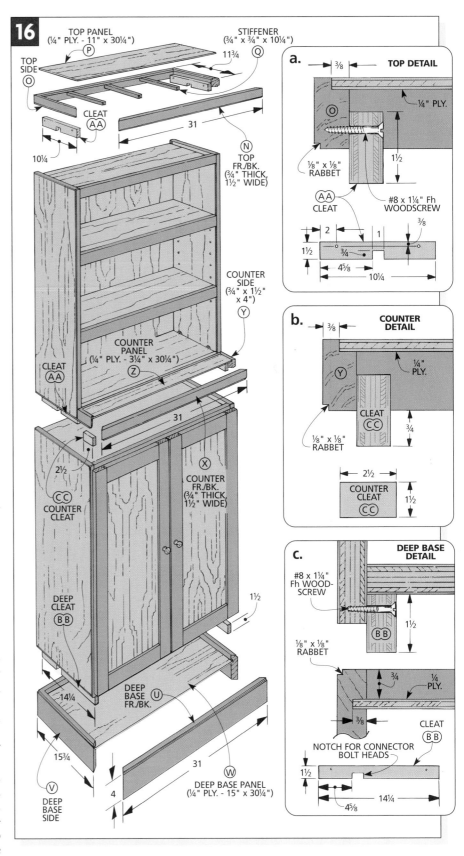

TECHNIQUE . . . . . . Shop-Made Edging

Veneer edging tape is a convenient way to cover a plywood edge. But the grain and color of the tape doesn't always match the color of your plywood. This was the case when I built the modular wall cabinets.

To solve this problem, I tried something a little different. I made edging strips by removing the thin layer of veneer from leftover plywood used on the project. This way the color matches, and it's easy to cut additional edging strips as they're needed.

Making your own edging isn't as difficult as it sounds, but it does take a few steps. First, I cut the pieces about $1/8$" wider than the edges to be covered; see Step 1. Then I ripped the veneer from these pieces; see Step 2.

Next, I used my belt sander to remove the thin layer of core material that's left on the back side of the veneer; see Step 3. (Shop Note: You have to be a little careful here since the veneer on most hardwood plywood is only $1/32$" or less in thickness. Check often on your progress. If you're not paying attention, it's easy to sand right through the veneer.)

Finally, the edging can be glued to the plywood with a couple coats of contact adhesive. I like to start on the ends (Step 4) and then apply veneer across the front; see Step 5.

Since the edging is cut extra wide, it needs to be trimmed flush with the plywood face; see Step 6. The edging is so thin that a sanding block makes fast work of getting the veneer edges down flush with the panel.

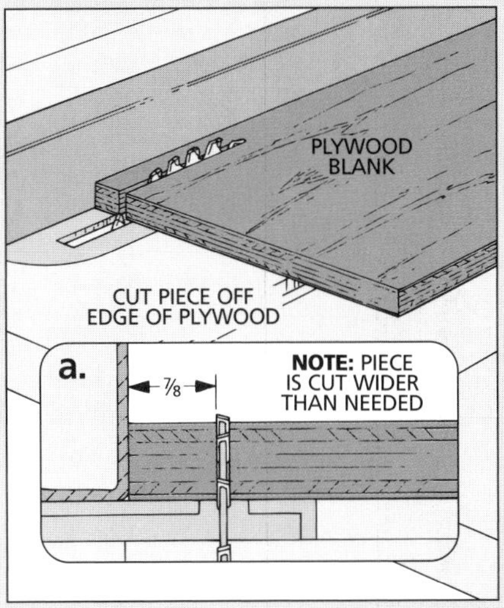

1 *To begin, rip a 7/8"-wide piece from a plywood blank. This extra width allows the veneer strip to overhang the edges of the plywood.*

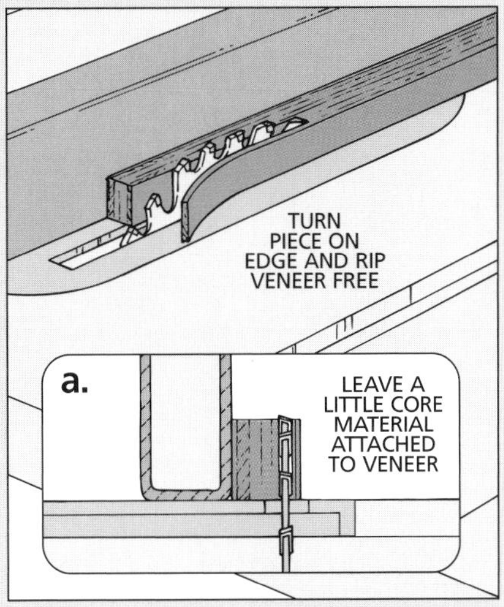

2 *Now, to cut the veneer free, turn the piece on edge. Set the rip fence to remove the veneer and about 1/32" of the core material.*

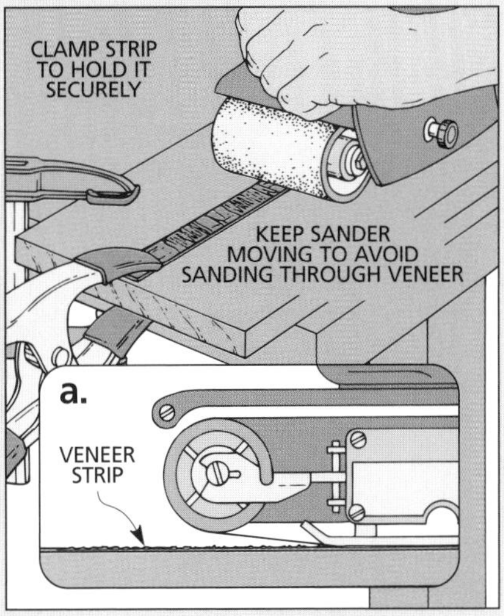

3 *A belt sander makes quick work of removing the core material from the veneer. I clamp the strip to a backing board to hold it in place.*

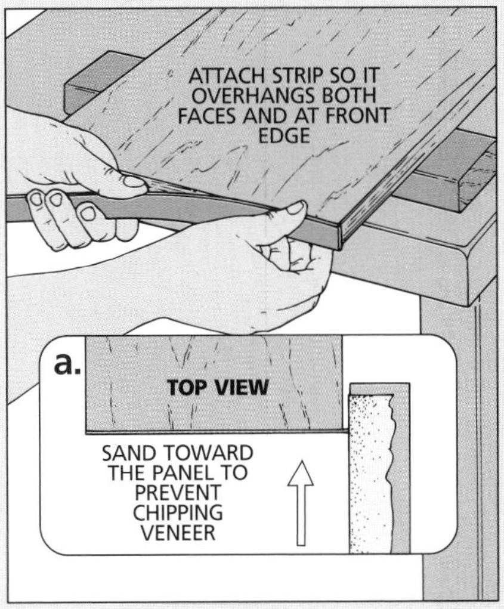

4 *To attach the edging on the ends of the plywood, I use two coats of contact adhesive. Then I sand the ends flush with a sanding block.*

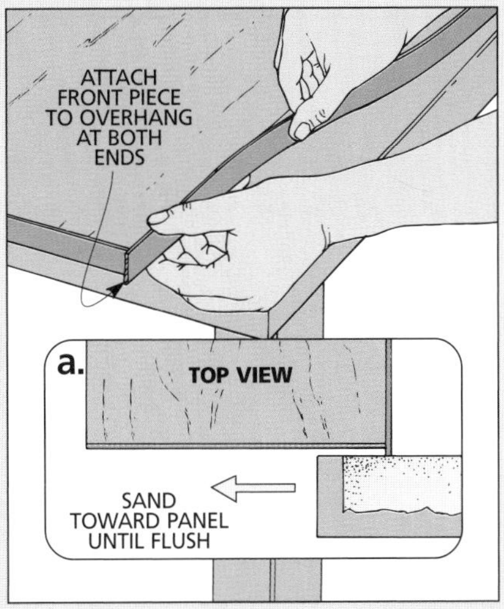

5 *With the side pieces flush, the veneer is glued across the front the same way. Overlap the ends, then sand the veneer flush with the ends.*

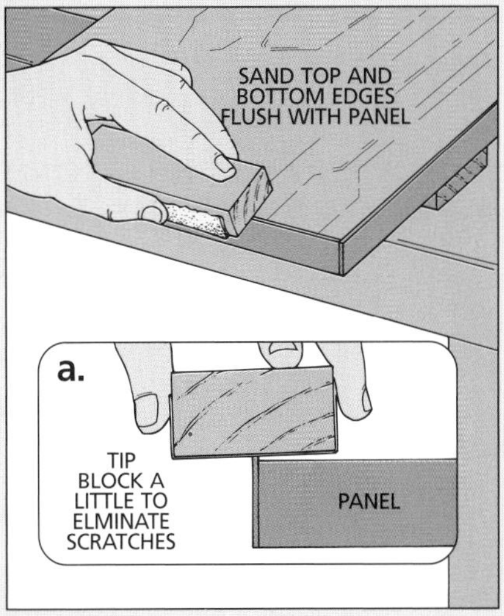

6 *To trim the edges of the edging, sand them lightly with a sanding block. Tip the sanding block very slightly to avoid cross-grain scratches on the plywood.*

What's the most difficult part of mounting doors on a cabinet? I think it's getting the hinges positioned correctly. If you're even a *little* off, the door will fit crooked on the cabinet.

The beauty of European-style hinges like those used on the modular cabinets on page 45 is that they're easy to mount and adjust. If the doors are even slightly crooked or out of alignment with each other, you can easily adjust the hinges to get everything lined up perfectly.

Adjustment is just a matter of loosening an adjustment screw, repositioning the door, and then retightening the screw; see below. The door can be adjusted up to $1/8''$ in three ways — side-to-side, in-and-out, or up-and-down. (I've noticed that most people will see an up-and-down misalignment first so pay special attention to that.)

TWO-PART HINGES. These hinges come in two parts. The actual hinge has a round cup on the bottom that fits into a 35mm (or $1^3/8''$) hole (mortise) drilled into the door. Then a separate mounting plate is screwed inside the cabinet. On

some European hinges you slide the two parts together and then tighten them with the turn of a locking screw. On the Blum hinge shown in the photo at left, the hinge snaps on and off the mounting plate. You don't even need a screwdriver.

FINAL ADJUSTMENT. I like to install the hinges and plates in my shop and get the doors so they are roughly positioned. But I wait to make the final adjustments until the cabinet is set up in its final position. Then it's easy to line everything up and retighten the screws.

STYLES. European hinges are available in a variety of styles depending on the design of your door and cabinet. You can find them in full overlay (shown here), half overlay, or inset. Most have a self-closing feature so you don't need additional catches. For sources of European hinges, see page 95.

Adjusting European Hinges

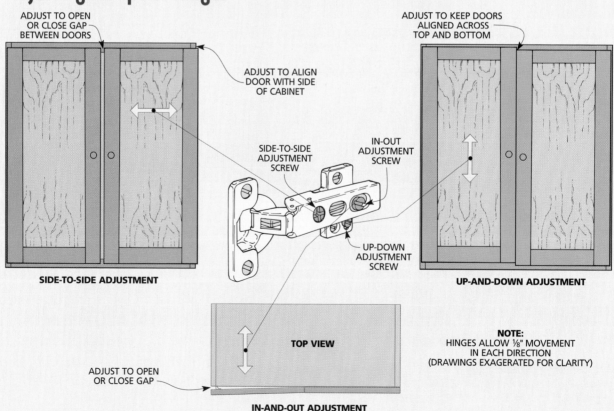

ADJUST TO OPEN OR CLOSE GAP BETWEEN DOORS

ADJUST TO ALIGN DOOR WITH SIDE OF CABINET

ADJUST TO KEEP DOORS ALIGNED ACROSS TOP AND BOTTOM

SIDE-TO-SIDE ADJUSTMENT SCREW

IN-OUT ADJUSTMENT SCREW

UP-DOWN ADJUSTMENT SCREW

SIDE-TO-SIDE ADJUSTMENT

UP-AND-DOWN ADJUSTMENT

TOP VIEW

ADJUST TO OPEN OR CLOSE GAP

IN-AND-OUT ADJUSTMENT

NOTE:
HINGES ALLOW $1/8''$ MOVEMENT IN EACH DIRECTION (DRAWINGS EXAGERATED FOR CLARITY)

Installing European Hinges

When it came time to install the European hinges on the modular cabinets, I found it easiest and most accurate to make a simple jig; see drawing at right.

MAKING THE JIG. The jig is built in a giant "I" shape. I cut the center (vertical) piece from some scrap 3/4" stock. The length matches the height of the doors.

Next I screwed on a pair of horizontal "wings" made from 1/4" hardboard. The bottom edge of the top wing and the top edge of the bottom wing indicates the centerline of the hinges and plates. For the modular cabinet this measurement is 4" from the top and bottom of the door.

REFERENCE LINES. Once the jig was screwed together I added a few reference lines. First add a couple of lines to the center piece 3/4" from the top and bottom ends. These will indicate the *inside* (top and bottom) of the cabinet; see Step 3.

Then add reference lines on the wings 2 1/2" from the center piece. These indi-cate the back screw location of the mounting plate. By marking both sides of the wings, you can use the jig for the left or right side of the cabinet.

Note: The locations of the mounting plate screws and location and depth of the hinge mortises can vary from one European-style hinge to another. This depends on the manufacturer and design of the hinge. The measurements given here are for Blum 125° full-overlay snap-on hinges (No. B075M555).

USING THE JIG. Once the jig is complete, you can use it to lay out the location of the mortises on the stiles; see Step 1. Then the 35mm (or 1 3/8") mortises can be drilled on the drill press; Step 2.

Now use the jig to mark the location of the mounting plate (Step 3). Then install the mounting plate (Step 4) and the hinge (Step 5). Finally, snap the hinge and the plate together and add the last two screws (Step 6).

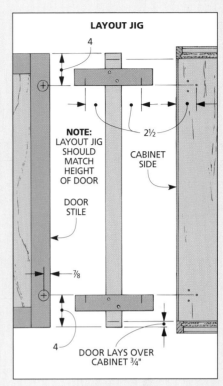

LAYOUT JIG

4

NOTE: LAYOUT JIG SHOULD MATCH HEIGHT OF DOOR

CABINET SIDE

DOOR STILE

2 1/2

7/8

4

DOOR LAYS OVER CABINET 3/4"

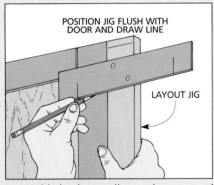

POSITION JIG FLUSH WITH DOOR AND DRAW LINE

LAYOUT JIG

1 *Hold the layout jig so the top and bottom ends align with the top and bottom of the door. Then mark a center-line for the hinges on the door stile.*

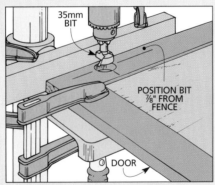

35mm BIT

POSITION BIT 7/8" FROM FENCE

DOOR

2 *Clamp a fence to the drill press table 7/8" from the center of the bit. Then drill a 1/2"-deep hole. (Note: These mea-surements may vary; see note in text.)*

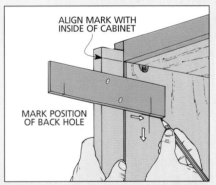

ALIGN MARK WITH INSIDE OF CABINET

MARK POSITION OF BACK HOLE

3 *Hold layout jig in the same position as the final position of the door. Then mark centerlines for the back screw of mounting plates on inside of the cabinet.*

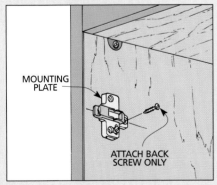

MOUNTING PLATE

ATTACH BACK SCREW ONLY

4 *Now screw the mounting plate to the inside of the cabinet with the back screw only. (The other screws will be added later.)*

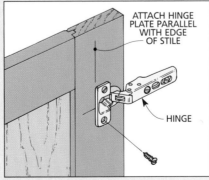

ATTACH HINGE PLATE PARALLEL WITH EDGE OF STILE

HINGE

5 *Position the hinge in the round mor-tise drilled in the door stile so the plate is parallel with the edge. Then screw it in place with two screws.*

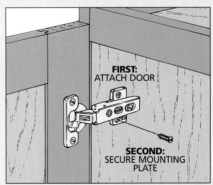

FIRST: ATTACH DOOR

SECOND: SECURE MOUNTING PLATE

6 *Now snap the hinges and mounting plates together. Finally, add the last two screws in the plate and adjust the doors as explained on the opposite page.*

CORNER CABINET

With glass, raised-panel doors, and shop-made moldings this classic country cabinet will enhance any corner of a home.

Corner cabinets usually involve a lot of angled cuts and complex joinery. Typically, you would try to figure out all the angles first, then build the case, and finally add the shelves. But to make construction easier, I did it backwards.

I made the shelves and top and bottom first, and then built the sides of the cabinet around them. This way you can lay out and cut the angles on flat pieces.

JOINERY. The design of this cabinet also keeps any complex joinery to a minimum. There are long splines that join the sides and front stiles. But the rest of the case is simply screwed together. The screws are all hidden by moldings.

MOLDINGS. That brings up another thing I like about this project. You can combine a number of simple moldings (that are cut on the router and table saw) and come up with what looks like rather complex base and top moldings. For example, the top crown molding has a cove that's an easy cut on a table saw.

DOORS. One more thing should be mentioned about the design. I added glass upper doors and raised panel lower doors.

On the top half I was faced with building doors with small panes — including the top panes which had to be cut in an arc to match the top door rail.

To simplify all of this, I took a different approach. The glass in each door is just one big rectangular pane. Then the horizontal muntins (dividers) lay on top of the glass, but they're still tied into the door stiles with an offset mortise and tenon joint. This way the only arc you have to cut is on the top rails of the door, not the glass.

EXPLODED VIEW

OVERALL DIMENSIONS:
$79^{3}/_{8}$H x $44^{3}/_{8}$W x $16^{1}/_{8}$D

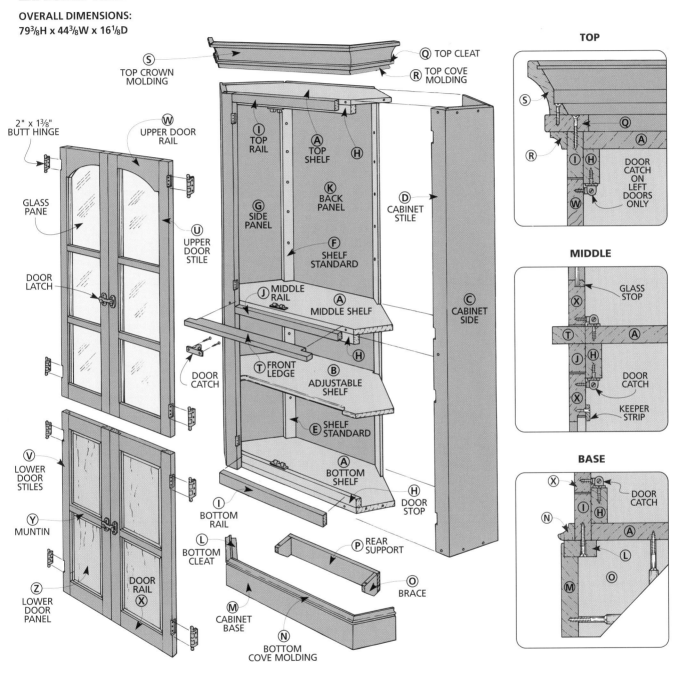

S — TOP CROWN MOLDING
Q — TOP CLEAT
R — TOP COVE MOLDING

2" x $1^{3}/_{8}$" BUTT HINGE
W — UPPER DOOR RAIL
GLASS PANE
DOOR LATCH
U — UPPER DOOR STILE

I — TOP RAIL
A — TOP SHELF
H
K — BACK PANEL
G — SIDE PANEL
F — SHELF STANDARD
D — CABINET STILE

J — MIDDLE RAIL
A — MIDDLE SHELF
C — CABINET SIDE

T — FRONT LEDGE
B — ADJUSTABLE SHELF
H
DOOR CATCH
E — SHELF STANDARD

V — LOWER DOOR STILES
Y — MUNTIN
Z — LOWER DOOR PANEL
DOOR RAIL X

A — BOTTOM SHELF
H — DOOR STOP

I — BOTTOM RAIL
L — BOTTOM CLEAT
M — CABINET BASE
N — BOTTOM COVE MOLDING
P — REAR SUPPORT
O — BRACE

TOP

S
R
I H W
Q
A
DOOR CATCH ON LEFT DOORS ONLY

MIDDLE

X
T
J
X
A
GLASS STOP
H
DOOR CATCH
KEEPER STRIP

BASE

X
N
I H
A
M
L
O
DOOR CATCH

MATERIALS. I built the corner cabinet out of straight-grained Ponderosa pine (C and Better grade). The pine, gives the project a classic country look. Since the back is made from $1/_{4}$" plywood (and pine plywood isn't commonly available), I used birch plywood for the back.

If you were to build the cabinet with a hardwood such as cherry or oak, it would take on a traditional, formal look. Then plywood should be used that matches the rest of the cabinet.

FINISH. One of the problems with finishing pine is that it can get blotchy when it's stained. To prevent this, I brushed on a coat of Minwax Wood Conditioner before staining. Then I stained with a coat of Minwax's Early American finish.

Finally, I brushed on two coats of McCloskey's Heirloom (eggshell) Varnish and rubbed it smooth with "000" steel wool.

MATERIALS LIST

A	Top/Mid./Btm. (3)	³⁄₄ x 13³⁄₈ - 40¹⁄₂
B	Adjust. Shelves (3)	³⁄₄ x 13³⁄₈ - 40¹⁄₂
C	Cabinet Sides (2)	³⁄₄ x 7¹⁄₄ - 72
D	Cabinet Stiles (2)	³⁄₄ x 2¹⁄₂ - 72
E	Shelf Std. (Btm) (2)	³⁄₄ x 1³⁄₄ - 30¹⁄₄
F	Shelf Std. (Top) (2)	³⁄₄ x 1³⁄₄ - 39¹⁄₂
G	Side Panels (2)	¹⁄₄ ply - 12 x 72
H	Door Stops (3)	³⁄₄ x 1¹⁄₂ - 32⁵⁄₈
I	Top/Btm. Rails (2)	³⁄₄ x 2 - 26³⁄₄
J	Middle Rail (1)	³⁄₄ x 1¹⁄₄ - 26³⁄₄
K	Back Panel (1)	¹⁄₄ ply - 23¹⁄₂ x 72
L	Btm. Cleat (1)	³⁄₄ x 1¹⁄₂ - 60
M	Cabinet Base (1)	³⁄₄ x 4¹⁄₈ - 60

N	Btm. Cove Mld. (1)	³⁄₄ x ³⁄₄ - 60
O	Braces (4)	³⁄₄ x 4¹⁄₄ - 4¹⁄₄
P	Rear Support (1)	³⁄₄ x 4¹⁄₄ - 23¹⁄₄
Q	Top Cleat (1)	³⁄₄ x 2 - 60
R	Top Cove Mld. (1)	³⁄₄ x ³⁄₄ - 60
S	Top Crn. Mld. (1)	³⁄₄ x 3 - 60
T	Front Ledge (1)	³⁄₄ x 1¹⁄₂ - 29
U	Upper Dr. Stiles (4)	³⁄₄ x 2 - 38¹⁄₄
V	Lower Dr. Stiles (4)	³⁄₄ x 2 - 27³⁄₄
W	Upr. Rails (Top) (2)	³⁄₄ x 4¹⁄₂ - 11³⁄₈
X	Dr. Rails (6)	³⁄₄ x 2 - 11³⁄₈
Y	Muntins (6)	³⁄₈ x ³⁄₄ - 11³⁄₈
Z	Lwr. Dr. Panels (4)	³⁄₄ x 9⁷⁄₈ - 11⁷⁄₈

HARDWARE SUPPLIES
(86) No. 6 x ³⁄₄" Fh woodscrews
(10) No. 8 x 1" Fh woodscrews
(46) No. 8 x 1¹⁄₂" Fh woodscrews
(32) ⁵⁄₈" Brads
(2) ¹⁄₈" Glass (cut to fit)
(8) 2" x 1³⁄₈" Brass butt hinges
(4) Adjustable brass door catches
(2) Brass door latches
(12) Pin-type shelf supports

CUTTING DIAGRAM

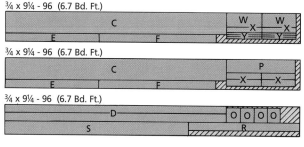

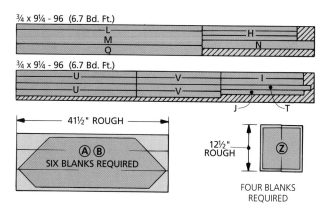

NOTE: ALSO NEED ONE 4' x 8' SHEET OF ¹⁄₄" PLYWOOD FOR THE SIDE (G) AND BACK (K) PANELS

ALSO REQUIRED: Pieces A, B, and Z are cut from glued-up blanks, see drawings at right. You need nine 1x6's (³⁄₄ x 5¹⁄₂ x 96) (36 bd. ft.) to make all the blanks.

Gluing-Up Panels

When edge-gluing panels, the easiest step to rush through is selecting the wood. But carefully choosing and arranging the boards are essential.

Selecting straight boards makes clamping much easier. Some *slight* warp is unavoidable and can be corrected. A warped board can be ripped in two or forced flat while clamping.

After selecting the lumber, I cut the pieces to size. (Note: I don't usually include pieces *wider* than 5" in an edge-glued panel.) Then I arrange the boards as they will be in the panel.

It's like a puzzle. First, I turn and flip the pieces until the color and grain patterns seem to match.

Next comes grain direction. After the panel is glued up, you'll need to plane it smooth. If the grain on the boards runs in opposite directions, some pieces might chip out while planing. To determine the grain direction, look at the *edge* of the board; see Fig. 1. You may have to pick the direction it curves the most.

There's one more thing to consider in solving the puzzle — how will the panel cup (warp) with

changes in humidity? To minimize the cupping, I like to alternate the end grain from board to board; see drawing above.

Okay, so which of the criteria is most important: appearance, grain direction, or end grain? For me it's appearance. I try to get the grain direction and end grain arranged correctly as well, but often, it becomes a compromise.

Once the boards are arranged into a panel, I chalk Roman numerals across the joints to keep them in order while they're being prepared; see Fig. 2.

ORIENTING END GRAIN IN SAME DIRECTION CAN CAUSE CUPPING AS PANEL DRIES

ALTERNATING END GRAIN HELPS KEEP PANEL FLAT

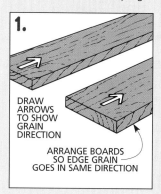

1.
DRAW ARROWS TO SHOW GRAIN DIRECTION
ARRANGE BOARDS SO EDGE GRAIN GOES IN SAME DIRECTION

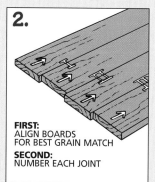

2.
FIRST: ALIGN BOARDS FOR BEST GRAIN MATCH
SECOND: NUMBER EACH JOINT

TOP, BOTTOM, AND SHELVES

I started work on the corner cabinet by making the top, middle shelf, and bottom (all labeled A), and the three adjustable shelves (B). All six pieces are made by edge-gluing $3/4$"-thick stock to make blanks $13^3/8$" wide by $40^1/2$" long. (Note: After the case is built, the adjustable shelves are re-cut slightly and notched to fit in the case.)

LAYOUT. Once the blanks are made, you can begin laying out the angles that give these pieces (and eventually the cabinet) their shape; see Fig. 1. (Shop

Note: I layed out and cut one blank. Then, I used that blank as a template to mark the others.)

Begin the layout by drawing a center line on the blank; see Fig. 1. Then make reference marks on the front edge $15^9/16$" on both sides of the centerline.

Next, place a combination square along one end to lay out a 45° angle from the reference mark on the front edge to the end of the blank; see Fig. 2. (In my case, this line measured $6^5/8$" long; see Fig. 1.)

Then flip the combination square over so it points toward the back edge

and lay out another line at a 90° angle from the first line.

CUT OUT SHAPE. After the lines are laid out on both ends, you can cut out the finished shape. I did this with the miter gauge set at a 45° angle on the table saw.

ADJUSTABLE SHELVES. On the three adjustable shelves, I cut a relief on the front edges; see Fig. 1. (This makes room for the keeper strips on the back of the lower doors.) Then I routed a plate groove (this is optional) along the back edges of two of these shelves (B). (See box below.)

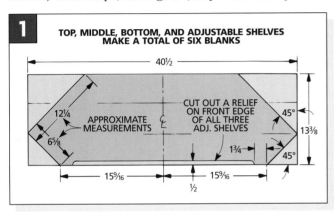

1 TOP, MIDDLE, BOTTOM, AND ADJUSTABLE SHELVES
MAKE A TOTAL OF SIX BLANKS

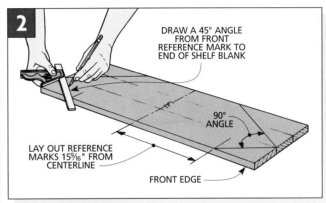

2 DRAW A 45° ANGLE FROM FRONT REFERENCE MARK TO END OF SHELF BLANK

Plate Groove

After making the adjustable shelves for the corner cabinet, I decided to rout what's called a "plate groove" along the back edges of two of the shelves. This groove holds plates upright to display them.

After some tests, I found that a $1/2$" core box bit routs the best groove. When the groove is centered 2" from the back edge, it holds plates at a nice angle.

The challenge was to figure out a way to rout a plate groove that turns the corners and runs along all three back edges. I did this by mounting a guide bushing to the base of my router and used the bushing to follow a $1/4$" hardboard template that's firmly clamped to the top of the shelf; see drawing.

Shop Note: Router guide bushings are designed to follow a template. They fit around the bit and screw to the bottom of the router base; see detail in drawing. You can buy bushings for your specific router from many mail order catalogs (see page 95), or you can buy a universal base with bushings.

The trick when using this technique is figuring out the exact size of the template. Since I wanted the plate groove to be centered 2" from the back edge of the shelf, the template had to be cut at least 2" short of the back of the shelf.

But you also have to take into consideration the diameter of the guide bushing. In this case I used a bushing with a $5/8$" outside diameter

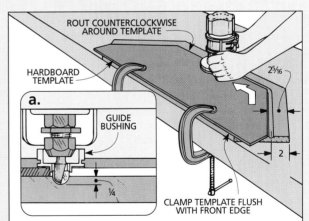

($5/16$" radius). This meant I had to cut the template a total of $2^5/16$" short of the back edges of the shelf.

After making the template, I clamped it flush to the front of the shelf and $2^5/16$" from the back.

Next, mount the guide bushing and bit in the router and lower the bit so it takes

a $1/4$"-deep cut.

Once everything is set up, rout in a counterclockwise direction around the template. To rout a smooth, "burn-free" groove, press the bushing up tight against the template. Make one continuous pass and don't slow down while routing.

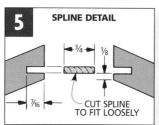

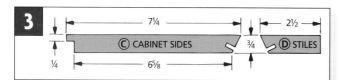

SPLINE DETAIL

CUT SPLINE TO FIT LOOSELY

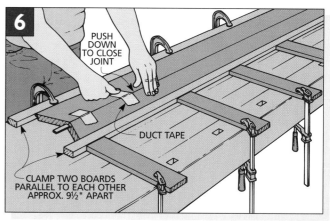

PUSH DOWN TO CLOSE JOINT

DUCT TAPE

CLAMP TWO BOARDS PARALLEL TO EACH OTHER APPROX. 9½" APART

SIDES AND STILES

Once the top, bottom, and shelves are all cut to shape, work can begin on the cabinet sides and stiles (the vertical pieces on the front of the cabinet). These pieces are joined together with a spline joint.

CUT TO SIZE. Start by cutting two cabinet sides (C) and two cabinet stiles (D) to a common length of 72". Then rip one edge of each piece to create a 22½° bevel. Now, cut the cabinet sides (C) to a width of 7¼", and the stiles (D) to a width of 2½"; see Fig. 3.

RABBET. Before cutting the spline joint, I cut a rabbet along the back edge of the cabinet sides (C) to accept the side panels (G). Cut this rabbet so the distance from the short end of the bevel to the rabbet matches the length of the angled front edges on the top and bottom pieces (A). (In my case, this was 6⅝"; see Figs. 1 and 3.)

SPLINE JOINT. The purpose of the spline between the sides (C) and the stiles (D) is to help align the pieces when gluing. (It doesn't add significant strength to the joint.)

To make the joint, start by cutting a ⅛" kerf into the bevels on the edges of both the cabinet sides (C) and stiles (D). I did this by tilting the blade to 22½° and running the pieces through the saw on edge (with the bevels down); see Fig. 4.

Then cut a spline to fit loosely within the kerf; see Fig. 5. (Shop Note: The spline could be ⅛" hardboard, but if it fits too tight, assembly will be difficult. Also, the spline can be a series of pieces, not one 72"-long piece.)

ASSEMBLING THE JOINT. To help assemble the joint, I clamped a couple of straight boards to my bench parallel to each other and about 9½" apart; see Fig. 6. Then I wedged a cabinet side (C) and stile (D) together between the straight boards (with the spline in place). When pressure is applied on top of the pieces the joint closes up. (Test clamp this setup dry before gluing. The distance between the straight boards may need adjusting).

Once the joint is tight down its length, glue it up and hold the pieces down with several strips of duct tape while the glue dries; see Fig. 6.

ASSEMBLY

I found it easiest to assemble the case while it was on its back; see Fig. 7.

ATTACH FRONT ASSEMBLY. Position the top and bottom pieces flush with the ends of the front assembly (C,D), and the middle shelf 39½" down from the top piece. Then screw through the front stiles (D) and into the top and bottom pieces (A); see Fig. 7.

Next, add two screws along the top and bottom of the sides (C). The screws will be hidden later by the top and base moldings. But that's not the case with the middle shelf. There I just used one screw through the front stile and into the middle shelf (¾" in from the inside edge of the stile); see Fig. 8. It will be covered later by a front ledge.

SIDE PANELS. Once the front pieces are screwed down, turn the case over and measure for the ¼" plywood side panels (G). Cut the width of the side panels ¾" less than the distance from the inside of the rabbet to the back corner; see Fig. 8.

After the side panels are cut to size, they can be screwed down; see Fig. 8a.

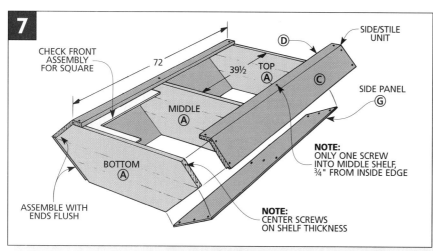

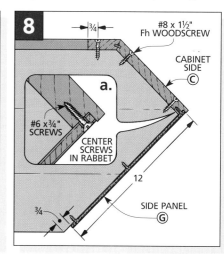

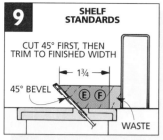

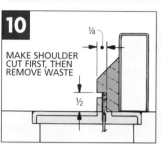

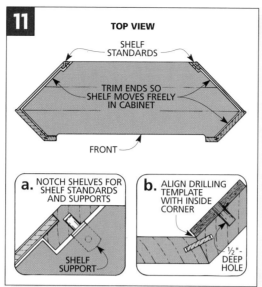

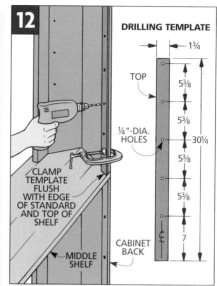

SHELF STANDARDS

The shelves are supported by shelf supports that fit into holes drilled in shelf standards and in the case; see Fig. 12.

CUT STANDARDS. Start by cutting the four shelf standards to fit in the top and bottom sections of the case. In my case, the two bottom standards (E) were $30\frac{1}{4}$" long and the two top standards (F) were $39\frac{1}{2}$" long.

Next, cut a 45° bevel off one edge of all four standards (to fit against the back of the cabinet) and then trim them to a common width of $1\frac{3}{4}$"; see Fig. 9. Now cut a rabbet opposite the bevel to fit around the side panel; see Fig. 10.

ATTACH STANDARDS. After the rabbets are cut, glue the standards to the inside of the cabinet; see Fig. 11a.

DRILLING TEMPLATE. I found the easiest way to keep all the pin support holes aligned was by making a drilling template; see Fig. 12. To make the template, cut a piece of $\frac{1}{4}$" plywood to the same width and length as the bottom shelf standard (E). Then drill $\frac{1}{4}$" holes centered on the width and positioned as shown in Fig. 12.

Now, with the template clamped so it sits on the top of the shelf, drill through each hole until there's a $\frac{1}{2}$"-deep hole in the shelf standard; see Fig. 12.

After drilling holes in each of the standards at the back of the cabinet, I used the template to drill matching holes on the inside of the cabinet at the front of the cabinet. Align the edge of the template on the joint; see Fig. 11b.

NOTCH SHELVES. Once all of the holes are drilled, notch the three adjustable shelves (B) to fit around the standards. Then trim the ends slightly so the shelves will fit around the supports; see Fig. 11a.

STOPS AND RAILS

The next step on the cabinet is to add the door stops, rails, and a front ledge.

STOPS. There are three door stops (H) — one at the top of the upper section and two in the lower section. Start by ripping the stops $1\frac{1}{2}$" wide. Determining the length of the door stops is a little tricky. The stops fit behind the stiles (D), and I wanted to bevel both ends at 45° to match the

angle inside the cabinet; see Fig. 13. The distance between the short points of the bevel has to match the distance from one spline joint (on the inside) to the other spline joint.

After the stops are cut to length, they can be glued in place behind the cabinet stiles (D); see Figs. 13, 14, and 15.

RAILS. Next, cut the three rails. The top and bottom rails (I) are cut to a width of 2". But the middle rail (J) is cut $1\frac{1}{4}$" wide since there's a $\frac{3}{4}$" front ledge added above it; see Fig. 15a.

To determine the length of the rails, measure the distance between the cabinet stiles (D). (In my case, $26\frac{3}{4}$".) After they're cut to length, glue the rails to the front of the stops. The top and bottom rails (I) are mounted flush with the top and bottom of the cabinet; see Figs. 13a and 14a. But the middle rail (J) is aligned with the *bottom* of the middle shelf; see Fig. 15a.

FRONT LEDGE. Next, add a front ledge (T) to the front of the middle shelf; see Fig. 15. First, cut it $1\frac{1}{2}$" wide and 29" long. Next, cut notches on both ends so it fits between the cabinet stiles. Then glue it to the front of the shelf.

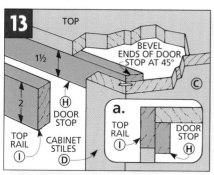

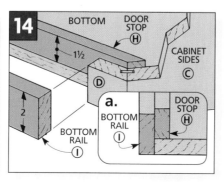

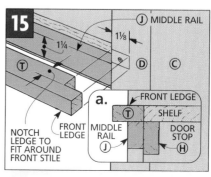

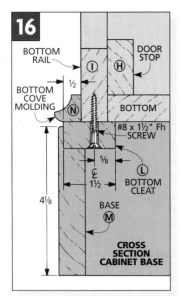

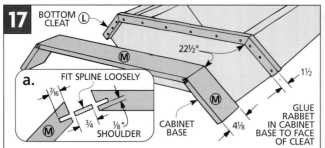

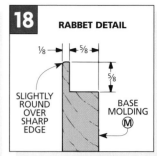

BASE

The base of the cabinet is built using a number of pieces; see Fig. 16. I started by screwing cleats (L) to the bottom of the cabinet to provide a mounting surface for the base.

CLEAT. Begin by cutting the cleats (L) to a width of $1^1/2$" and rough length. Then miter both ends of the *middle* cleat at $22^1/2°$ so the ends align with the joints of the stiles and sides, (see Fig. 17), and it sticks out $1/2$" from the front of the cabinet; see Fig. 16.

After the middle cleat is cut to length, miter the front end of each side cleat and then cut the back end to length (at 90°).

BASE. After the cleats were screwed down, I added the base pieces (M) to the front. These three pieces have a rabbet cut on the top edge to fit around the cleats; see Fig. 18. After cutting the rabbet, miter the pieces so the miters align with the miters on the cleats.

To join the base pieces, I used a spline joint (like the sides and stiles); see Fig. 17a. Then I glued the base pieces to the cleats.

COVE MOLDING. The last step on the base is to add the cove molding (N). To make the molding, first rout $1/2$" coves along both edges of a $2^1/2$"-wide by 36"-long blank; see Fig. 19, Step 1. While I was set up, I routed two pieces this size to make enough molding (R) for the cabinet top as well.

Then round over the bottom edge of the *bottom* cove molding only; see Step 2. Finally trim the $3/4$"-wide molding off both edges; see Step 3.

Now miter the molding to fit around the cabinet and glue it in place on top of the cleats; see Fig. 16.

SUPPORT BRACES

To add strength to the base of the cabinet, I screwed triangular braces (O) behind the base pieces. Two of the braces fit behind the front base piece and the other two support a rear support; see Fig. 21.

CUT TO SIZE. Start by cutting four braces $4^1/4$" square. Then trim one corner off at 45° leaving 1" shoulders along two edges; see Fig. 20.

To fit around the bottom cleats (L),

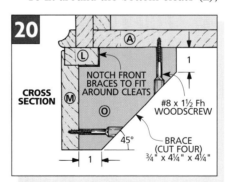

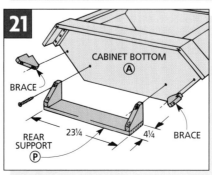

cut notches out of the two front braces; see Fig. 20. Then screw two of the braces to the back of the base piece (M) and to the bottom of the cabinet.

REAR SUPPORT. The back of the cabinet is held up with a rear support (P); see Fig. 21. Cut it to the same width as the braces ($4^1/4$") and to the same length as the back edge of the cabinet bottom ($23^1/4$" in my case). Then screw the back braces onto the inside face of the rear support. Now screw this assembly to the bottom of the cabinet.

TOP MOLDING

The top molding is made from a combination of pieces fastened together.

TOP CLEAT. Begin by making and screwing down three top cleats (Q) just like the bottom cleats; see Fig. 24. The top cleat is a little different though. It's 2" wide and is mounted so it sticks out 1" in front of the cabinet; see Fig. 24.

COVE MOLDING. Next, cut the cove molding (R) (made earlier) and glue it underneath the cleats; see Fig. 24.

CROWN MOLDING. To make the crown molding, I started by cutting two blanks $3^1/2$" wide. Then cut one to a rough length of 36" (for the front) and one 24" (for the two sides).

To cut the wide cove on the face of the moldings, clamp a straightedge fence to the saw at a 30° angle to the blade; see Fig. 22. Position the fence so the top of the blade is centered on the width of the blank. Now cut the cove by making light passes, increasing the blade height between passes until the cove is $1/4$" deep.

Next, rip the blank so *one* edge is ⁵/₈" from the cove; see Step 1 in Fig. 23. Then make two cuts on this edge with the blade set at 30°; see Steps 2 and 3.

Now lower the blade so it's only ¹/₄" high, and cut a slot on the back of the molding for a spline; see Step 4. Finally, cut off the other edge at 30°; see Step 5.

The last step is to cut a pocket for mounting screws. To make the pocket, cut a angled groove in the back of the molding with a dado blade; see Step 6.

MOUNT THE MOLDING. Now the molding can be cut to fit on top of the cleat; see box below.

To hold the joints together, I added splines shaped like elongated triangles into the slot in the molding; see Fig. 25.

BACK PANEL

The back panel (K) can now be cut from ¹/₄" plywood so it's the same height as the side panel (72"), but ¹/₂" narrower than the distance between the outside corners of the shelf standards (so the back won't stick beyond the sides); see Fig. 25. Then screw the panel into place.

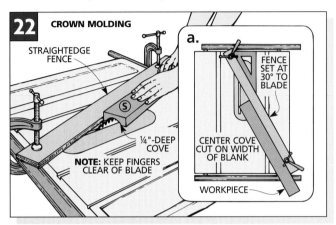

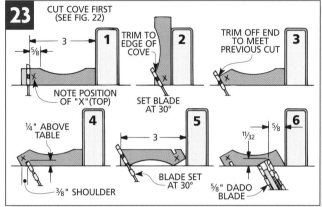

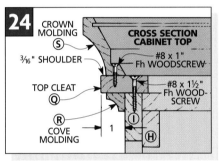

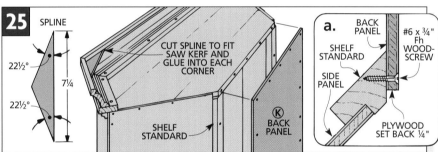

Mitering Crown Molding

Fitting crown molding around the top of a project usually means cutting a compound angle. One way to do this on a table saw is to angle the miter gauge and tilt the blade. These two angles are not that easy to figure out without referring to a chart.

But if the molding can be tilted to the angle it will be when attached to the project, the blade can stay at 90°, and only the miter gauge need be angled.

To do this, I screwed an auxiliary fence to the miter gauge. The auxiliary fence has to be high enough to

support the molding when it's standing up as it will appear on the corner cabinet; see detail in drawing.

The back of the molding has a ¹/₈" kerf cut in it. This kerf is intended to accept a spline when the top is assembled, but I found it can be used for another purpose.

If you slip a narrow strip of ¹/₈" hardboard in the kerf, and then hold the hardboard against the auxiliary fence, it helps support the molding in the correct position while it's being cut.

Now, to miter the crown molding, rotate the miter gauge to 22¹/₂° (this reads

67¹/₂° on some miter gauges). Then bring the molding tight against the auxiliary fence so the base of the molding is flat on the table. And make the cut.

To cut the other end of the

front piece, I just moved the miter gauge to the opposite slot and turned it to the opposite 22¹/₂° setting.

One end of each side piece is cut the same way, but it has a 90° cut on the other end.

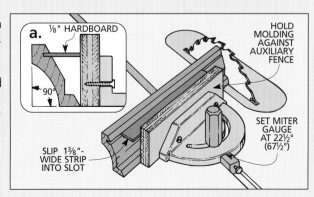

DOOR STILES

After the case of the cabinet was complete, I built the doors. I made glass upper doors and paneled lower doors. (You could leave off the upper doors.)

DESIGN CONSIDERATIONS. The basic construction of both the upper and lower doors is the same. They're built as open frames; see Fig. 26. Then I put one large pane of glass (or two raised panels) into rabbets in the back of each door. The glass and raised panels are held in place with stops and keeper strips; refer to Fig. 36.

To build the doors this way, I had to come up with a slightly different mortise and tenon joint; see Fig. 27. Since the muntins are mounted in front of the glass and panels, the joint for the muntins must be offset slightly towards the front. Once I was set up to cut these offset mortises, it was easiest to cut the mortises for all of the rails this way.

CUT OUT STILES. Start making the doors by cutting all of the stiles (vertical pieces) to a common width of 2" from $3/4$"-thick stock; see Fig. 28.

To determine the length of the stiles, measure the height of the cabinet openings. Cut the stiles (U, V) to length so the doors fit tight in the openings. Then after the doors were built, I planed them down for a uniform $1/16$" gap all around.

LAY OUT MORTISES. Next, lay out the location of the mortises along the inside edge of the stiles; see Fig. 28. The mortises for the rails are $1 1/4$" long. Those for the muntins are $1/2$" long.

CUTTING MORTISES. I cut the mortises on a drill press with a fence; see Fig. 29. (If you don't have a fence, clamp a straight board to your drill press table.)

To cut the mortises, first insert a $3/16$" brad point bit in the drill press and set the speed to about 2000-2500 RPM. Then tighten the fence down so it's $3/16$" from the inside edge of the bit. To get

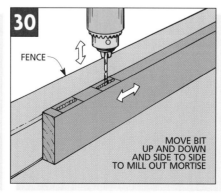

NOTE:
ALL DOOR STOCK
$3/4$" THICK EXCEPT
MUNTINS ($3/8$")

NOTE:
WHEN SIZING GLASS,
ALLOW $1/16$" CLEARANCE
ON ALL FOUR SIDES

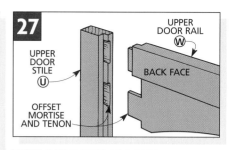

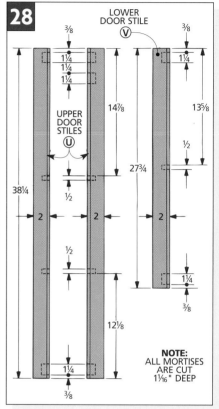

NOTE:
ALL MORTISES
ARE CUT
$1 1/16$" DEEP

the mortise to be offset toward the front of the stile, keep the *front face* of the stile against the fence. This will leave room for the $3/8$" rabbet on the inside face of the stile (refer to Fig. 31a).

To make the mortise, start by drilling holes at each end. Then drill a series of holes next to each other; see Fig. 29. (Don't overlap the holes or the bit can wander into the previous hole.)

After the initial holes are drilled, I went back and drilled out the areas between the holes. Finally, I used a "milling" action to clean out the remaining ridges; see Fig. 30. Rapidly raise and lower the bit while slowly moving the workpiece from side to side.

RABBET. After all of the mortises are cleaned out, rout a rabbet along the back edge of each stile; see Fig. 31.

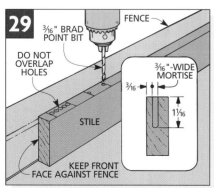

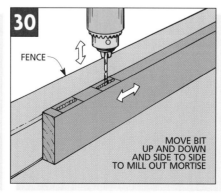

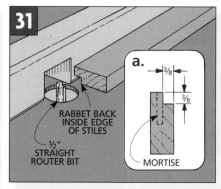

DOOR RAILS

Next, I made the rails and muntins. To determine their length, measure the distance between the *cabinet* stiles (D) and divide by two (for two doors). Then subtract 4" (for the two door stiles), and add 2" (for the 1" tenons on each end.)

Now, cut the two top upper door rails (W) $4\frac{1}{2}$" wide, the other six rails (X) 2" wide, and the six muntins (Y) $\frac{3}{4}$" wide.

The muntins are mounted so they're in front of the glass and raised panels. So they have to be resawn to $\frac{3}{8}$" thick.

CUTTING THE TENONS. To avoid confusion when cutting tenons, I marked the front and back face of all the pieces.

On the rails (but not the muntins) cut a $\frac{3}{8}$"-deep rabbet at the ends on the *back* face; see Fig. 33. Then, turn the rails over and cut a rabbet on the *front* face to create a tenon that fits the mortise; see Fig. 33. Also cut this same rabbet on the front face of the muntins.

Note that the rabbet on the front face is wider than the one on the back so it fits in the rabbet on the door stiles.

CUT TO WIDTH. To permit the tenons to fit in the mortises, trim the shoulders by cutting $\frac{3}{8}$" from the corner of the rails and $\frac{1}{8}$" on the muntins. Then cut a $1\frac{1}{4}$"-wide notch in the tenon on the top upper door rails to create two tenons; see Fig. 32. (Cut the notch to align with the inside shoulder.)

There's also a little area under the outside corner of each rail that has to be cleaned out with a chisel; see Fig. 32.

BACK RABBET. After all of the tenons fit the mortises, cut a rabbet on the back inside edges of all the rails (but not the muntins) to accept the glass or panels. This rabbet is $\frac{3}{8}$" wide on the six rails (X); see Fig. 32. However, the rabbet on

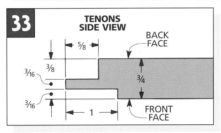

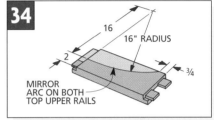

the two top upper rails (W) is $2\frac{7}{8}$" wide.

ARC ON TOP RAIL. Next, lay out and cut an arc on the bottom edge of the top upper door rails (W); see Fig. 34. Now assemble the doors checking for square.

PANELS, STOPS

To make the raised panels (Z) that fit in the lower doors, start by edge-gluing four panels. Then cut the panels to fit in the rabbets on the doors. (Don't fit them too tight. They may expand with changes in humidity.)

COVE. Now, rout a cove around the front edge of each panel; see Fig. 35. To do this, make a series of passes (move

the fence between passes) with a core box bit; see Fig. 35a.

KEEPER STRIPS. To hold the panels in place, I screwed keeper strips behind each panel; see Figs. 36b and 36c.

GLASS STOPS. To hold the glass in the doors, I made $\frac{1}{4}$"-thick stops. Miter the stops, and then tack them to the stiles; see Fig. 36a. (The notch along the edge of each stop makes it easier to remove if the glass should break.)

HINGE MORTISES. Before mounting the glass, I cut hinge mortises in the door and cabinet stiles, refer to Fig. 26.

HARDWARE. After applying the finish, mount the door catches and latch; see Exploded View on page 57. ■

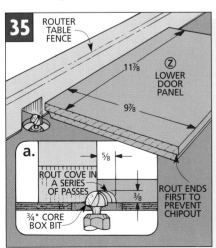

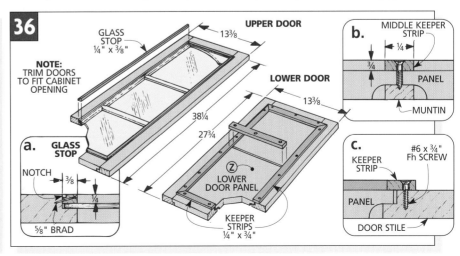

DISPLAY CABINET

The beauty of this project is its traditional appearance. But what you can't see is the unique technique used to build the doors.

The first thing you're likely to notice about this cabinet is the upper doors. Each door is neatly divided into eight glass "lights" or panes. And each pane is framed by a molded edge. But it's not the glass that intrigues me. What I find interesting is how the doors are constructed.

How are all those parts on the door joined together? And how do you cut the inside corners on the door moldings? There must be a lot of exact miters or coped corners to cut. Or at least an expensive set of router or shaper bits. (Not at all. It's a neat technique using a router with common bits. I explain how to do it on pages 74–75. And I strongly recommend you read these pages before you begin building the doors for the display cabinet.)

TOP MOLDING. The door is not the only part that has interesting details. The molding at the top of the cabinet is made by adding pieces of stock one on top of another. And one of those pieces is dentil molding — that's another intriguing story. It's cut to fit the width of the cabinet and the blocks are spaced to end up with a full block at each end.

WOOD. I used red oak to build the display cabinet. The doors, facings, molding, and shelves are all made of solid stock, but the main parts are made from oak plywood. I wanted the main parts to remain flat and stable even during changes in humidity.

HARDWARE. To make it easy to disassemble, I used threaded inserts to join the upper case to the lower case. And, to add a touch of class to the project, I chose decorative brass hardware.

FINISH. The final important detail to any heirloom project is the finish. For the stain I used 8 teaspoons of burnt umber artist's oil, mixed into 1 quart of linseed oil. Then after 48 hours I covered it with three coats of General Finishes' Royal Finish (Satin).

EXPLODED VIEW

OVERALL DIMENSIONS:
42 1/4W x 16D x 77 7/8H

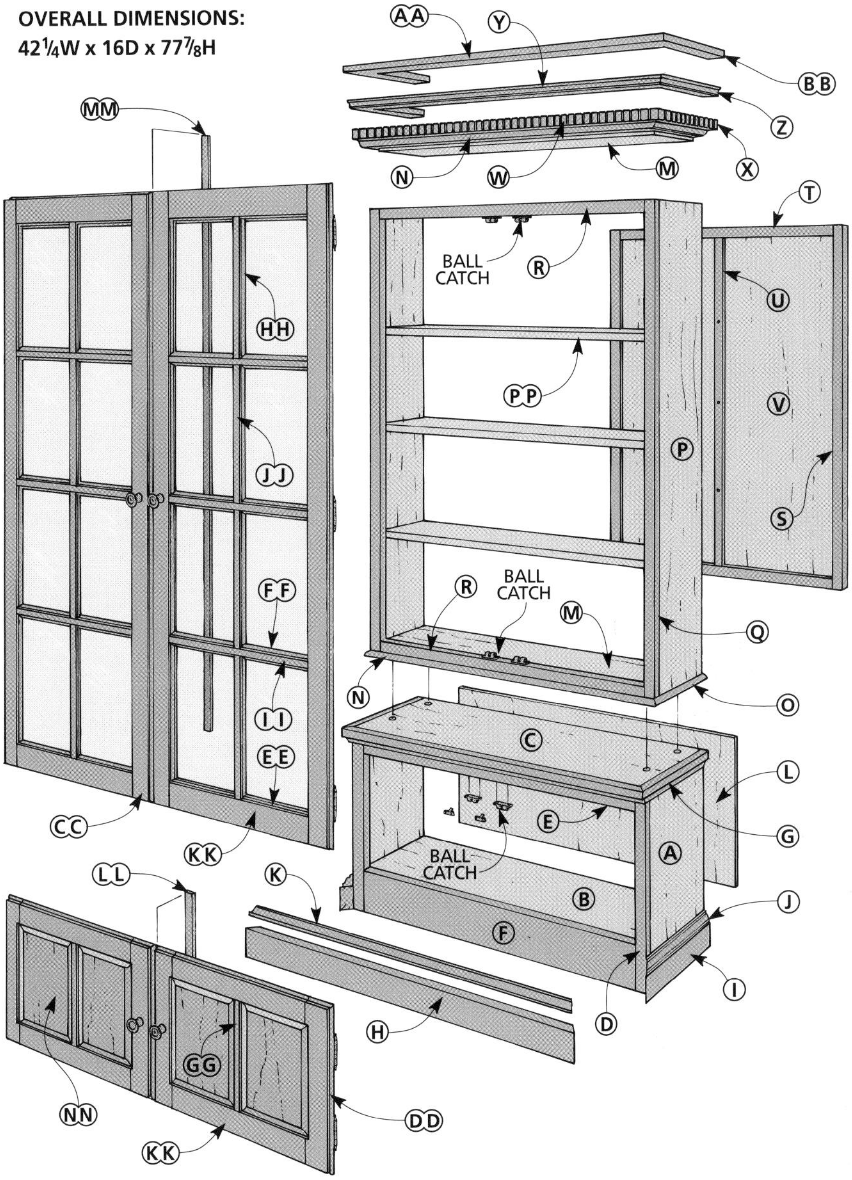

MATERIALS LIST

LOWER CASE		
A	Sides (2)	3/4 ply - 14 3/4 x 21 5/8
B	Shelf (1)	3/4 ply - 14 1/4 x 38 1/4
C	Top (1)	3/4 ply - 15 5/8 x 40
D	Side Facings (2)	3/4 x 1 - 21 5/8
E	Upper Rail (1)	3/4 x 1 3/4 - 37 1/4
F	Lower Rail (1)	3/4 x 4 3/4 - 37 1/4
G	Edging Strip (1)	3/8 x 3/4 - 75 rough
H	Kickbd. Front (1)	3/4 x 3 - 40 3/4
I	Kickbd. Sides (2)	3/4 x 3 - 16
J	Side Moldings (4)	3/4 x 1/2 - 16 rough
K	Frt. Moldings (2)	3/4 x 1/2 - 41 rough
L	Back (1)	1/4 ply - 38 3/4 x 22 1/8
UPPER CASE		
M	Top/Bottom (2)	3/4 ply - 11 1/4 x 37 3/4
N	Frame Fronts (2)	1/2 x 1 1/2 - 40 1/4
O	Frame Sides (4)	1/2 x 1 1/2 - 12 1/2
P	Sides (2)	3/4 ply - 11 1/2 x 52
Q	Side Facings (2)	3/4 x 1 - 52
R	Face Rails (2)	3/4 x 1 - 37 1/4
S	Back Stiles (2)	3/4 x 1 1/2 - 52
T	Back Rails (2)	3/4 x 1 1/4 - 36 1/4
U	Back Divider (1)	3/4 x 1 - 50
V	Back Panels (2)	1/4 ply -17 7/8 x 50
W	Dentil Front (1)	1 1/2 x 1 - 40 3/4
X	Dentil Sides (2)	1 1/2 x 1 - 12 3/4
Y	Front Trim (1)	3/4 x 1 1/4 - 41 3/4
Z	Side Trim (2)	3/4 x 1 1/4 - 13 1/2
AA	Front Cap (1)	3/4 x 1 1/2 - 42 1/4
BB	Side Caps (2)	3/4 x 1 1/2 - 13 1/2
DOORS		
CC	Upper Stiles (4)	3/4 x 2 1/2 - 50 1/2
DD	Lower Stiles (4)	3/4 x 2 1/2 - 15 5/8
EE	Rails (8)	3/8 x 2 1/4 - 14 1/2
FF	Horiz. Dividers (6)	3/8 x 1/2 - 14 1/2
GG	Lr. Ver. Dvdrs. (2)	3/8 x 1/2 - 15 5/8
HH	Up. Ver. Dvdrs. (2)	3/8 x 1/2 - 50 1/2
II	Horiz. Caps (6)	3/8 x 1 - 14 1/4
JJ	Vert. Caps (10)	3/8 x 1 - 11 1/8
KK	Rail Caps (8)	3/8 x 2 1/2 - 14 1/4
LL	Lower Astragal (1)	3/8 x 3/4 - 14 7/8
MM	Upper Astragal (1)	3/8 x 3/4 - 49 3/4
NN	Panels (4)	5/8 x 6 7/8 - 11 1/8
OO	Glass Stop	1/4 x 1/4 - 70 Lin. Ft.
PP	Shelves (3)	3/4 x 10 1/4 - 37 3/4

HARDWARE SUPPLIES

- (25) No. 6 x 3/4" Fh woodscrews
- (67) No. 8 x 1 1/4" Fh woodscrews
- (4) No. 8 x 1 1/2" Fh woodscrews
- (14) No. 8 x 2" Fh woodscrews
- (5 pairs) Inset brass hinges with screws
- (4) 1/4" Threaded inserts
- (4) 1/4" x 1 1/4" Rh machine screws
- (4) Brass knobs
- (6) Double ball catches
- (15) 1/4" Shelf supports
- (16) 1/8" Glass panes - 6 7/8" x 11 1/8"

CUTTING DIAGRAM

3/4 x 7 1/2 - 96 (5 Bd. Ft.)

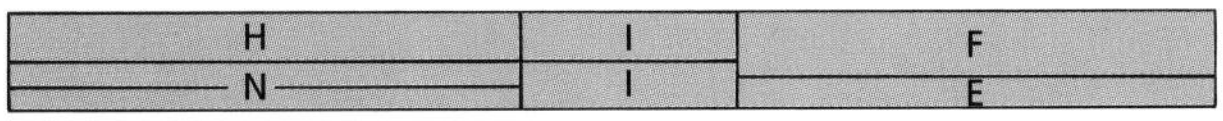

3/4 x 7 1/2 - 96 (5 Bd. Ft.)

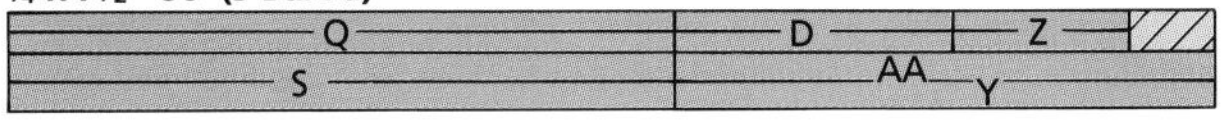

3/4 x 7 1/2 - 96 (5 Bd. Ft.)

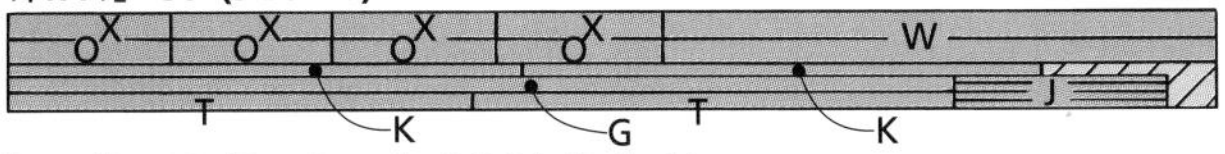

3/4 x 7 1/2 - 96 (Two Boards @ 5 Bd. Ft. Each)

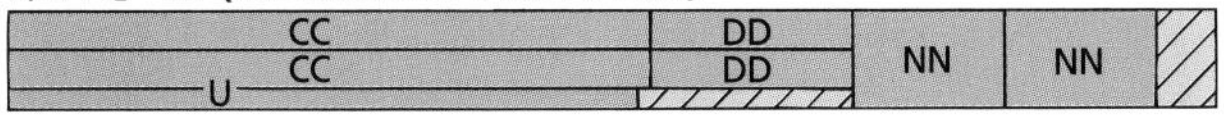

3/4 x 7 1/2 - 96 (Two Boards @ 5 Bd. Ft. Each)

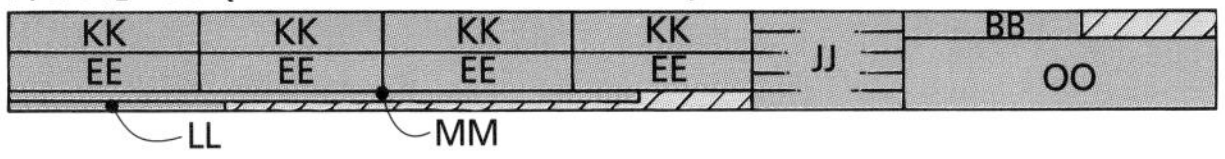

3/4 x 7 1/2 - 96 (Three Boards @ 5 Bd. Ft. Each)

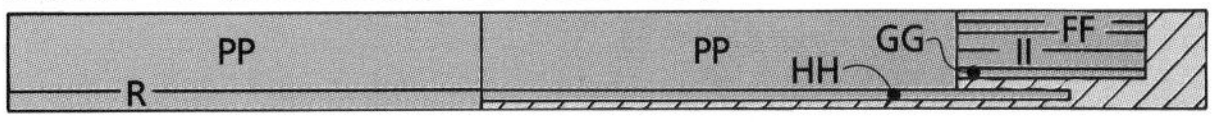

3/4" PLYWOOD 48 x 96

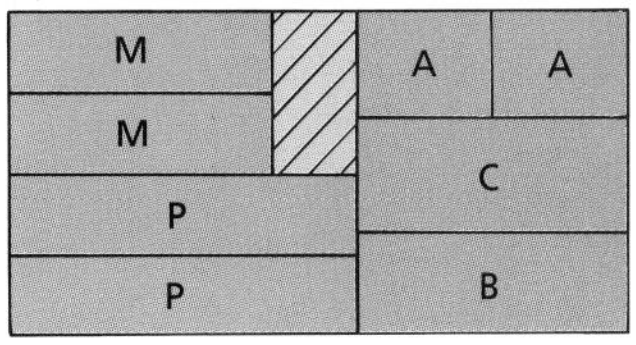

1/4" PLYWOOD 48 x 96

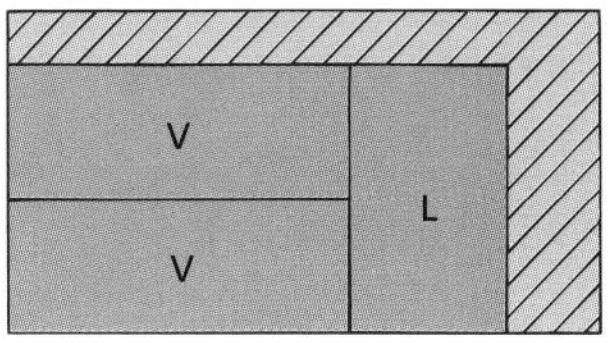

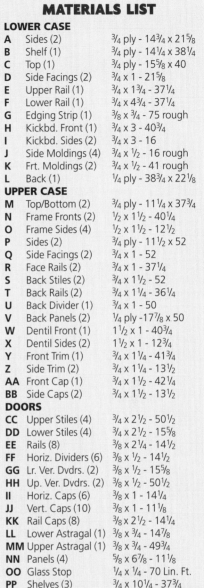

LOWER CASE

The display cabinet is constructed by stacking a tall case on top of a short case. I used plywood for the sides and backs, and then I covered the exposed front edges with solid wood strips.

Adding a kickboard and some molding strips gives the lower case the appearance of having a base without having to go through all the extra work that's needed to actually build one.

I began work on the cabinet by building the lower case. It starts out with two sides that are mirror images of each other. The sides are joined by a shelf to form an "H" shape, and then a top is added to help hold the assembly together; see Fig. 1.

SIDES AND SHELF. Start by cutting the two sides (A) and shelf (B) from $3/4$"-thick plywood; see Fig. 1. (Note the grain direction. I think it looks best if it runs vertically on the sides and along the length of the shelf.)

DADO FOR SHELF. After the sides and shelf have been cut to finished size, cut a $1/4$"-wide dado across the inside face of each side piece. These dadoes will receive tongues cut on the ends of the shelf; see Fig. 1. (Why not just eliminate the tongues and cut the dadoes wide enough to match the thickness of the shelf? There are a couple of reasons; see the box in the upper right-hand corner of this page.)

To cut the dadoes, you can use either a table saw with a dado blade or a $1/4$" straight bit on the router table. To allow the shelf to pull up tight to the side during assembly, cut the dadoes slightly deeper than $1/4$"; see lower photo in the box at upper right-hand corner.

TONGUES. Now you can cut the tongues on the shelf (B) to fit the dadoes. The tongues are formed by cutting two rabbets on each end of the workpiece; see Fig. 1b.

To do this I mounted a $1/2$" straight bit in the router table. Then I cut the tongues in a couple of passes, sneaking up on the final depth until the tongue just fit the dado in the side panels.

After the tongues have been routed on the ends of the shelf, rout a tongue the same size on the front edge of each side (A); see Fig. 1. These tongues will hold facing pieces added later; refer to Fig. 3 on opposite page.

CASE TOP. Once the tongues have been routed on the sides, the next step is

Tongue & Dado Joint

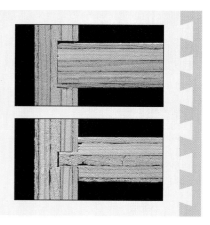

There are several ways to join a shelf to the side of a cabinet. A full-width dado (upper photo) works fine, but if the shelf doesn't fit exactly, there will be a visible gap.

The tongue and dado joint (lower photo) looks better because it hides any gap above the tongue of the shelf. It also covers up any splintering along the edges of the dado.

to cut the top (C) to finished size; see Fig. 1. (Again, note the grain direction.)

RABBETS FOR BACK. Now rabbets can be cut along the back edge of the sides (A) and top (C) to accept a back panel. Cut the $1/4$" rabbets on the *inside* face of the sides (the same face as the shelf dado) and *bottom* of the top panel; see Figs. 1 and 1a. Note: Don't cut a rabbet on the back edge of the shelf — the back

extends all the way to the floor.

HOLES IN TOP. There are two sets of holes to be drilled in the top (C) before the case can be assembled. First, drill and countersink a series of $3/16$" shank holes near each end for woodscrews that hold the top to the sides; see Figs. 2 and 2a. Then drill four $5/16$" holes for bolts that will be used to hold the top case to the bottom case; see Fig. 2.

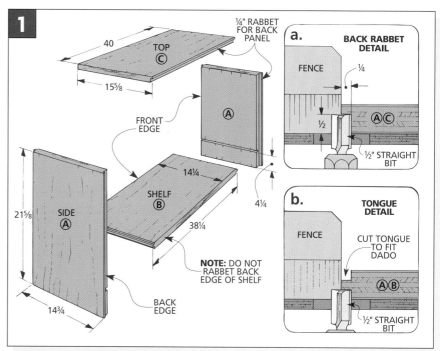

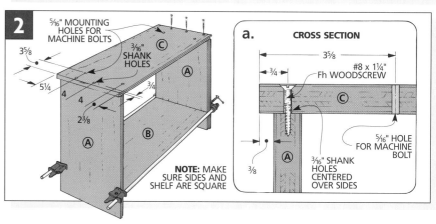

ASSEMBLY. The lower case is assembled in two steps. First, glue and clamp the shelf in the side dadoes to form an "H" shape; see Fig. 2. Then check to make sure the case is square.

Next, position the top (C) on the sides (A) so that it overhangs each side equally and is flush along the back. Then glue and screw the top down through the pre-drilled holes; see Fig. 2a.

FACING AND RAILS

The next step on the lower case is to add the facing pieces to the side panels, and to add the rails between each facing.

SIDE FACING. First rip two side facing (D) pieces to final width (1"); see Fig. 3a. Then cut the pieces to the same length as the sides; see Fig. 3.

Next, cut a groove on the back side of each facing to fit the tongues on the plywood; see Fig. 3a. (To make sure they fit the tongues, I used the same dado setup I used for the shelf dado.) Then glue the facings in place.

UPPER AND LOWER RAIL. Cut an upper rail (E) and a lower rail (F) to fit between the facings; see Fig. 3. Glue and screw the upper rail under the top (C). Then glue the lower rail to the shelf, and screw it to the facing; see Fig. 3b.

MOLDING AND KICKBOARD

Next I added edging strips, a kickboard, and molding to give the lower case a finished look. All three are mitered and cut flush with the back.

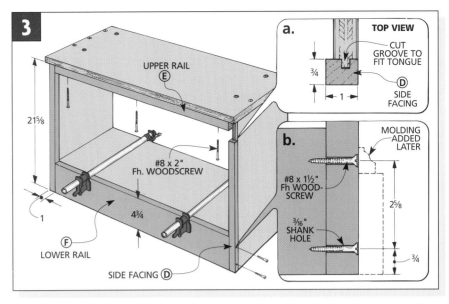

EDGING STRIP. To hide the edges of the plywood top, I glued ³/₈"-thick edging strips (G) to the front and sides; see Fig. 4. Start by ripping a blank to match the thickness of the top. Then rough cut the strip into three pieces.

Next, miter both ends of the front strip to length to fit across the front edge of the plywood; see Fig. 4. Then glue it in place. Now miter the front ends of the side strips, and cut the back ends flush with the back. Then glue these strips in place.

KICKBOARD. To make the kickboard, rip three pieces of ³/₄"-thick stock to width and rough length; see Fig. 4. Next, miter the kickboard front (H) and kickboard sides (I). To complete the kickboard, cut the back edges flush with the back. Then glue and clamp the pieces to the lower case.

ROMAN OGEE. I added strips of Roman ogee molding to the top edge of the kickboard and under the top of the lower case; see Fig. 4. The safest way to make this molding is to start with wider pieces; see Fig. 5a. (I used 1¹/₄"-wide blanks.) Rip enough stock to make four side molding strips (J) and two front molding strips (K).

Next, rout a Roman ogee profile on the outside edge of each strip. Then rip the molding ¹/₂" wide; see Fig. 5a. Cut the molding strips to length, then glue and clamp them in place; see Fig. 5.

BACK. A back panel (L) is all that's needed to finish the lower case. Measure between the rabbets on the sides, and between the rabbet on the top and the floor. Cut the back to size, then screw it in place; see Fig. 4.

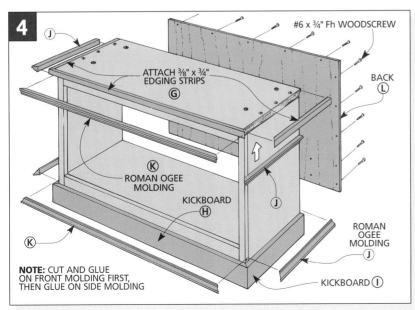

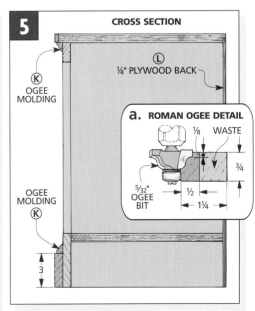

UPPER CASE

The upper case is built much like the lower case, but the shelves aren't permanently fixed to the sides.

TOP/BOTTOM. The top and bottom (M) are identical. Each one is a 3/4" plywood panel framed on three sides. Start by cutting the plywood panels to finished size; see Fig. 6.

Next, to accept the frame pieces, cut a groove centered on the front and side edges of the plywood; see Fig. 6a. Then cut a 3/4"-wide rabbet on the back edge of each panel for the back; see Fig. 6b.

TOP/BOTTOM FRAME. Now the frame pieces can be added. The frame fronts (N) and side (O) pieces are only 1/2" thick. Since the plywood is 3/4" thick, a rabbet will be formed when these frame pieces are glued to the panels; see Fig. 6. This rabbet will accept the sides and front faces of the case.

After cutting the frame pieces to width, rout a 1/2" roundover on one edge on each piece; see Fig. 6a. Then cut a rabbet on the *opposite* edge, to create a tongue that fits the groove in the top/bottom (M).

The next step is to miter the frame pieces to fit the panels; see Fig. 6. Then cut the ends of the frame sides (O) flush with the back edge of each panel.

THREADED INSERTS. After gluing the frame in place, install threaded inserts in the bottom panel to connect the two cases; see Fig. 8a. To locate the inserts, center the bottom panel on top of the lower case, making sure the back edges are flush. Then mark through the holes drilled in the top (C) of the lower case.

SIDES. Now you can start on the two sides (P). First cut two pieces of 3/4" plywood to final dimensions; see Fig. 7. Cut tongues for the facing (Q) on the front edge of each panel, and a rabbet for the back frame on the *inside* back edge of each panel; see Figs. 7a and 7b.

ASSEMBLY. To assemble the case, drill holes through the top/bottom assemblies; see Fig. 8. Then glue and screw them to the sides (P); see Fig. 8a.

SIDE FACING. To hide the edges of the side panels, glue a 1"-wide face frame to the upper case. To do this, first cut two side facings (Q) to length to fit between the top/bottom (M) panels; see Fig. 8.

Next, cut a groove on the back face of each side facing (Q) to fit the tongue on the front edge of the sides (P). Then glue the facing to the sides; see Fig. 8.

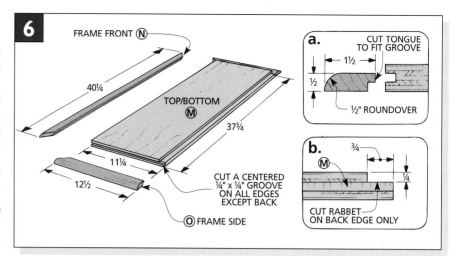

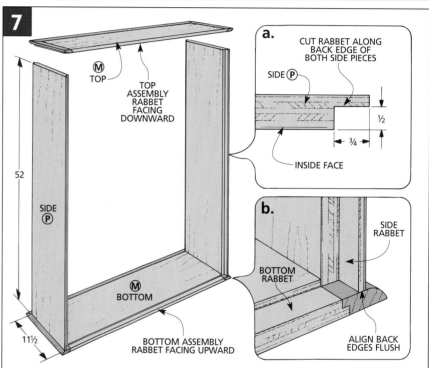

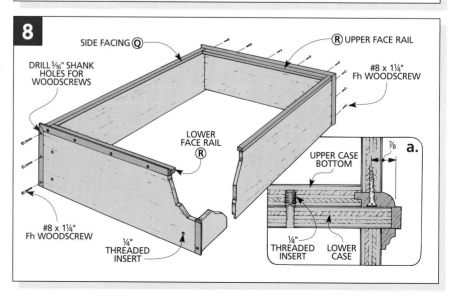

FACE RAILS. Now cut two 1"-wide face rails (R) to fit between the side facings; see Fig. 8. Then glue and screw them down to the frame front pieces (N).

BACK FRAME

Building the back is the next step in completing the upper case. It consists of two $1/4$" plywood panels in a frame, joined with stub tenons and grooves.

FRAME. To build the frame, first rip the stiles (S), rails (T), and divider (U) to final widths; see Fig. 9. (Notice they're all different widths.)

To determine the rough length of these pieces, measure the opening in the back of the cabinet (from rabbet to rabbet), and add 1". For now, cut the pieces to this rough length.

Next, cut a groove centered on the inside edge of each piece to accept the plywood back panels (V); see Fig. 9a. (Note: $1/4$" plywood may be slightly less than $1/4$" thick.) Cut grooves on both edges of the center divider (U).

Now the pieces can be cut to length. First, cut the stiles to fit the height of the opening (52"), and dry clamp them in place. To determine the length of the rails (T), measure the distance between the stiles (S) plus the depth of both grooves; see Fig. 9.

After the rails are cut to length, dry clamp them in place. Determine the length of the vertical divider (U) by using the same procedure as for the rails.

STUB TENONS. Now cut stub tenons on the ends of the rails (T) and divider (U) to fit the grooves; see Fig. 9a.

PANELS. Next, dry clamp the frame in the cabinet to determine the final dimensions of the back panels (V); see Fig. 9. Cut the panels from $1/4$" plywood, and glue the frame and panels together; see Fig. 9. Then glue and screw the back frame in place; see Fig. 9b.

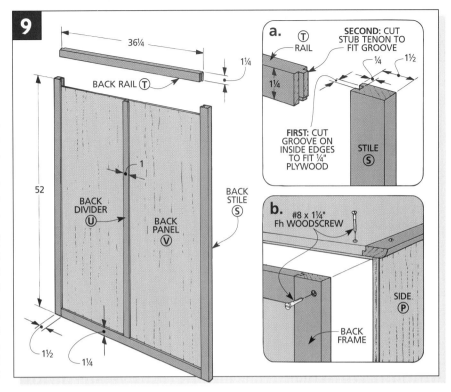

MOLDING

To finish off the upper case, I added molding to the top of the cabinet. The molding is built up out of three strips: a dentil molding, a Roman ogee molding, and a square edge cap; see Fig. 11.

DENTIL MOLDING. I wanted the blocks in the dentil to be equal in width and evenly spaced apart. I also wanted full blocks on both ends; see Fig. 10.

I made the blanks for the dentil front (W) and side (X) pieces from two pieces of $3/4$"-thick stock glued together; see Fig. 11a. (Or you could use a single piece of $1^1/2$"-thick stock.) After you're finished cutting dadoes for the dentils, miter the dentil pieces to fit around the front and sides of the cabinet; see Fig. 10. Then glue and screw them down securely to the case; see Fig. 11a.

TOP MOLDING. It's easier to make the $3/4$"-thick Roman ogee molding pieces and glue them to the front and side caps before cutting them to final length. To make the front (Y) and side (Z) Roman ogee moldings, rout a Roman ogee profile into the edge of $1^1/4$"-wide stock; see Fig. 11a (and refer back to Fig. 5a.).

Now you can cut the pieces for the front (AA) and side (BB) caps $1^1/2$" wide. Then glue and clamp the caps to the ogee trim pieces with the back edges flush; see Fig. 11a. After the glued-up pieces are dry, miter them to fit on top of the dentil molding.

CABINET ASSEMBLY. After the top molding is glued and screwed in place, set the upper case on top of the lower case. Then fasten the two cases together using $1/4$" machine screws to fit the threaded inserts.

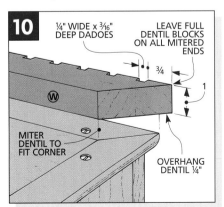

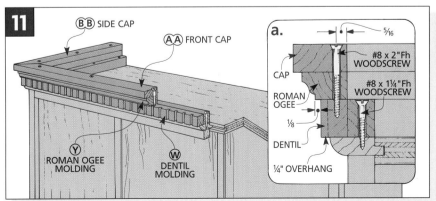

DOORS

I think the doors offer the biggest challenge on this whole project. (For an explanation on joining the door parts, see pages 74–75.)

DOOR STILES. To determine the lengths of the stiles (CC, DD), first measure the height of the door openings. Then add $1/2$" since the doors are lipped with a $1/4$" overlap; see Fig. 12.

Next, cut a groove and round over the inside edge of each stile; see Fig. 12a.

DOOR WIDTH. To determine the length of the rest of the door pieces, start by measuring the width of the opening and divide this measurement in half for the two doors (in my case, $18 5/8$").

Now subtract half the gap you want between the two doors ($1/16$"). Then add the overhang for the inset hinges ($3/16$"). This made each door $18 3/4$" wide.

RAILS AND DIVIDERS. To determine the length of the rails (EE) and horizontal dividers (FF), lay out two stiles with the routed edges facing in as in the finished door ($18 3/4$" outside to outside); see Fig. 12. Now measure between the grooves.

After cutting the rails and horizontal dividers to this length, cut the tongues and dadoes on each; see page 75.

VERTICAL DIVIDERS. To determine the length of the vertical dividers (GG, HH), dry assemble the stiles and rails. Then cut the dividers to length and cut the tongues and half-lap joints; again, see page 75. Now glue and clamp the rails and dividers together.

CAPS. All the rails and dividers have a molded cap (II, JJ, KK) glued on top. The caps are rounded over on the top and coved on the ends to match the molded edges of the stiles and rails; see Figs. 13 and 13a. To determine the length of all the caps, measure your assembled door; once again, refer to page 75.

OVERHANG AND ROUNDOVERS. Once the door is completely assembled, rout a $3/8$" rabbet around the back edges of each door; see Fig. 14. This will form an over-hang and leave a gap between the door and the cabinet opening. Next, rout a $1/4$" roundover on the front edges of each door; see Fig. 14a.

ASTRAGALS. The next step is to add an astragal (LL, MM). That's the strip that hides the gap when the doors are closed. Glue it into the rabbet in the left door; see Figs. 14 and 14a.

HANG DOORS. Before installing the glass and panels in the doors, I positioned the hinges and drilled the hinge screw holes. (See box on opposite page.) When this was done, I removed the hinges to mount the glass and panels.

PANELS, STOPS, HARDWARE. To dress up the bottom doors, I made $5/8$"-thick raised panels (NN). They're "raised" on both faces with a $1/2$" core box bit; see Fig. 15a. Install the panels and glass with quarter-round glass stop (OO); see Fig. 15b. After the doors are rehung, install the knobs and door catches.

SHELVES. Finally, glue up and cut stock for three shelves (PP).

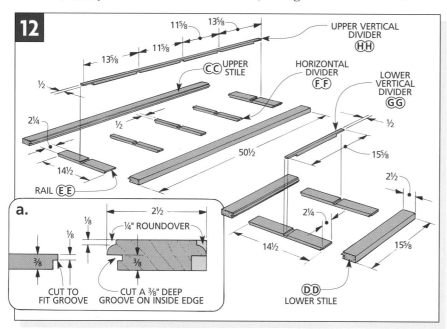

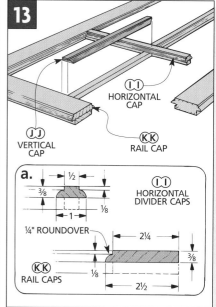

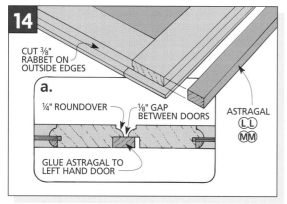

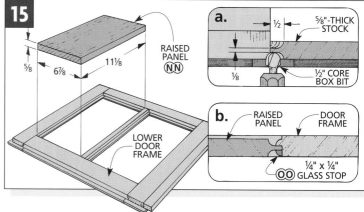

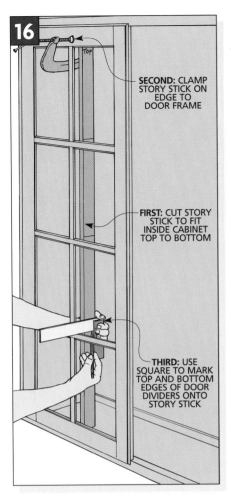

16

SECOND: CLAMP STORY STICK ON EDGE TO DOOR FRAME

FIRST: CUT STORY STICK TO FIT INSIDE CABINET TOP TO BOTTOM

THIRD: USE SQUARE TO MARK TOP AND BOTTOM EDGES OF DOOR DIVIDERS ONTO STORY STICK

SHELF POSITIONS

When there are shelves behind a glass door, I think it looks best if the shelves line up with the window dividers.

STORY STICK. To position the shelves, I used a story stick. This is simply a stick with holes drilled in it to mark the locations for the shelf support holes.

To make a story stick, first rip a piece of scrap wood to a width of 2″. Then cut this stick to length so it fits tightly up and down inside the cabinet. To keep everything straight, I labeled one end "TOP."

To get the holes on the story stick in the right place, temporarily clamp the stick to the door; see Fig. 16. Make sure the stick is straight up and down, and turn it so a narrow edge faces the front.

MARK DIVIDER EDGES. Then, use a try square to make two pencil marks on

the story stick that correspond to the bottom and top edge of each window divider; see Fig. 16.

MARK SHELF EDGES. Now, lay out the shelf positions on the stick; see Fig. 17.

MARK PIN LOCATIONS. The final thing to lay out on the story stick is the location of the holes for the shelf support pins. I used spoon-shaped pins; see Fig. 17a. (For different pins, adjust the position of the holes accordingly.)

By centering the hole on the width of the story stick, the hole will be the same distance from the edge when marking the front and back of the cabinet.

USING THE STICK. After holes are drilled through the stick for all the shelves, the stick can be used as a guide for drilling holes for the shelf supports.

The only secret to using the story stick is to keep the front edge of the stick flush to the inside edge of the cabinet when drilling the holes for the front pins. Then butt the opposite edge of the stick to the back of the cabinet when you drill the holes for the rear pins.

Note: To keep the shelves from sagging, I also put shelf pins in the vertical divider (U) in the back of the cabinet; see Exploded View on page 67. ∎

17

MARK EDGES OF DIVIDERS ONTO STORY STICK

ALIGN CENTER OF PIN HOLE WITH BOTTOM OF SHELF LINE

a.

SHELF SUPPORT PIN

LAY OUT SHELF THICKNESS CENTERED BETWEEN MARKS

Installing Inset Hinges

Inset hinges, like the ones used on this display cabinet, can be more frustrating to install than ordinary butt hinges. When the door is closed, both leaves of the hinge are inside the cabinet, making the screw holes in the hinge almost impossible to reach.

1. HINGE TO CABINET: To get around the problem, I installed the hinges before the glass was in place. And I used clamps to hold the hinges to the doors.

To do this, first screw all the hinges to the cabinet frame; see Fig. 1. Now put the doors in the opening

centered up and down and also left to right.

2. CLAMP TO DOOR: Then, to hold the doors in this position, I clamped the free leaf of each hinge to the door stile through the window opening; see Fig. 2. This way, the clamps hold the door securely in place.

3. HINGE TO DOOR: With a clamp on each hinge, open the door and drill pilot holes for the screws; see Fig. 3. (I used a Vix bit.) Then, screw in the screws and remove the clamps to check for fit. The screws can be removed and reinstalled after the glass is in place.

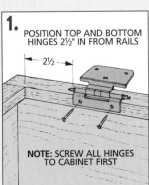

1.
POSITION TOP AND BOTTOM HINGES 2½″ IN FROM RAILS

2½

NOTE: SCREW ALL HINGES TO CABINET FIRST

2.
NOTE: POSITION DOORS IN CABINET, THEN CLAMP FREE LEAF TO DOOR STILE

LAY CABINET ON ITS BACK TO POSITION DOORS

USE SCRAP TO PROTECT DOOR FROM CLAMP

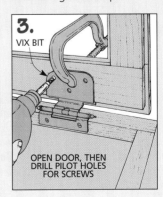

3.
VIX BIT

OPEN DOOR, THEN DRILL PILOT HOLES FOR SCREWS

When I see a well-built cabinet door with glass panes and wood dividers, I'll spend as much time looking at the coped and mitered joints as I do at what's on display behind it.

To build a door like this, you could either cut the coped miters by hand or use an expensive set of router bits. Instead, I use another technique for making matched molding joints. At first, it may look complicated (there are a lot of pieces), but it's not difficult.

The key to this technique is in the rails and dividers. Each consists of two separate pieces of wood (a $3/8$"-thick bottom divider or rail and a cap) glued together to look like one; see photo.

The advantage of this technique is that you can break down the operations into a number of simple steps. First, kerfs and a roundover profile are cut on the stiles; see below. Then tongues and half laps are cut on the bottom pieces; see next page. Finally, the ends of the caps are "coped" with a core box bit to match the roundover profile.

When all these pieces are glued up, the parts should mate perfectly. The tongue on the divider or rail fits into a groove cut in the stile. And the decorative roundover on the stile fits into the coped end of the cap like a nut in a shell.

Using this technique to build a divided door requires a few more pieces (and steps) than a typical door frame. To keep them all organized, I just take it a step at a time, starting with the stiles; see below. When they're finished, I move on to the dividers and then finally the caps.

EXPLODED VIEW

DIVIDER CAPS

HORIZONTAL DIVIDER

RAIL CAP

STILE

CAP

STILE

RAIL

RAIL/HORIZONTAL DIVIDER

VERTICAL DIVIDER

The Stiles

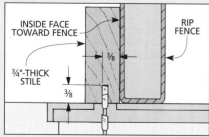

INSIDE FACE TOWARD FENCE

RIP FENCE

$3/4$"-THICK STILE

$3/8$

$3/8$

1 *Lock the rip fence $3/8$" from outside of the saw blade. Then, with the inside face of the stile against fence, cut a $3/8$"-deep kerf on the inside edge of the stile.*

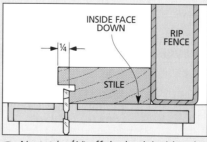

INSIDE FACE DOWN

RIP FENCE

$1/4$

STILE

2 *Next, trim $1/4$" off the back inside edge of each stile. Set height of blade to just cut into kerf. Position fence to let trimmed piece fall to waste side.*

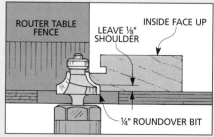

ROUTER TABLE FENCE

LEAVE $1/8$" SHOULDER

INSIDE FACE UP

$1/4$" ROUNDOVER BIT

3 *Use a $1/4$" roundover bit, and adjust height to leave $1/8$" shoulder. Then rout inside edge of each stile. (Save set-up for routing cap pieces.)*

The Dividers and Grid

The dividers and rails separate the glass panes and hold the frame together. Start by cutting tongues on the ends of each piece (Step 4). Then, half-lap joints are cut (Steps 5 and 6), and the pieces are assembled and glued to the stiles (Step 8).

To figure the length of the horizontal rails and dividers, begin with the final outside measurements of your door. Subtract the width of the two stiles, and add ¾" (for the ⅜"-deep kerfs that were cut on the stiles in Step 1). The vertical divider is the same length as the stiles.

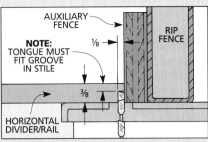

4 To cut the tongues on the dividers, clamp an auxiliary fence to the rip fence. Set fence ⅛" away from the outside of the blade, and make the cut.

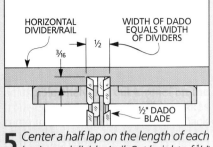

5 Center a half lap on the length of each horizontal divider/rail. Set height of ½" dado (or width of your dividers) to half the thickness of stock.

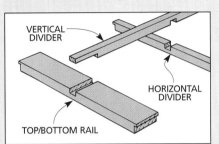

6 Cut matching half laps on vertical divider with same dado setup. End half laps at top and bottom are longer to fit wider top and bottom rails.

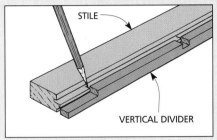

7 To help position horizontal dividers for assembly, use the vertical divider as a "story stick." Mark location of each half lap on back inside edge of the stile.

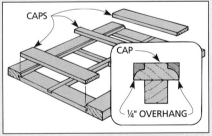

8 First, glue up the dividers and rails into a grid. Then glue stiles to the grid. To keep the corners flat, clamp a flat piece of wood across the stiles.

The Caps

Once the frame is assembled, the last steps are to add the caps and insert the glass panes or wood panels. The caps help to stiffen the frame and match the molding to the roundover on the stiles.

To determine the thickness of the caps, measure from the front face of the stile down to the grid (⅜" in my case).

In a divided door, the horizontal and vertical caps can't both run uncut. For a rigid door, I always span the shortest distance with the uncut cap. Then piece in the caps running in the other direction.

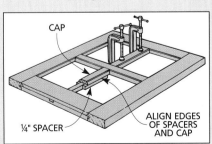

9 Rip caps to width allowing ¼" overhang on each edge (inside edge only for rail caps). The overhang forms a rabbet that holds glass or wood panel.

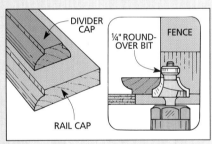

10 With height of router bit set the same as when routing the stiles, rout the profile on both edges of divider caps and inside edge of rail caps.

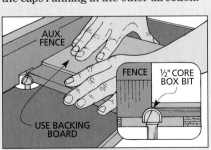

11 Cut ends of all cap pieces with ½" core box bit to match roundovers on mating pieces. Make trial cuts to determine height of bit and depth of cut.

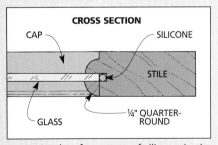

12 Position cap pieces on bottom grid, using a ¼" spacer as a gauge. Align edge of spacer with edge of cap. Then glue and clamp in place.

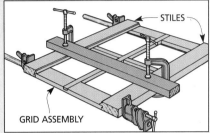

13 Apply a few spots of silicone in the grooves. The silicone will keep glass from moving sideways. Insert glass and secure with ¼" quarter-round.

GUN CABINET

This oak cabinet with dentil molding is a perfect place to display your rifles as well as keep them securely locked up.

W ith a few changes, the display cabinet plans on pages 66 – 73 can be modified to show off and secure a collection of rifles and ammunition. You can follow all of the instructions for building the display cabinet exactly until you come to the procedure for making the dividers for the upper doors on page 72.

UPPER DOORS. Here's where there's a change. To offer a better view of the rifles, I used a single sheet of glass without dividers in each door instead of eight panes. The stiles and rails remain the same as on the display cabinet.

LOCKS. Another change on the doors is to add locks to both the upper and lower cases; see the box on the opposite page.

TWO-PART RACK. The major change on the inside of the cabinet is the addition of a two-part rack to support guns; see Fig. 1. (But you won't have to build the shelves, part PP on the display cabinet.)

I based the dimensions for the rack on standard rifle barrels and butts; see Fig. 1. If you have a gun that's a little different, then you may have to modify your rack.

MATERIALS LIST

Use same Materials List, Cutting Diagram and Hardware as the Display Cabinet; see page 67. Omit pieces FF, HH, II, and PP.

ADDITIONAL PIECES NEEDED*

Barrel Rail (1) $3/4$ x $3 1/4$ - $37 3/4$
Rifle Base (1) $3/4$ x $10 1/2$ - $37 3/4$

*Cut from one board $3/4$ x $7 1/2$ - 96 (5 Bd. Ft.)

ADDITIONAL HARDWARE NEEDED

(3) No. 8 x $1 1/2$ " Fh woodscrews
(6) No. 8 x $1 1/4$ " Fh woodscrews
(2) Cam locks with keys and strike plates

BARREL RAIL

To build the barrel rail, first cut a piece of $3/4$"-thick stock to width; see Fig. 1. Then, to determine the length, measure the distance between the sides in the upper case.

After cutting the rail to length, cut three notches along the back edge of the barrel rail to fit around the stiles and divider in the back frame; see Fig. 1.

The barrels rest in notches cut in the front of the rail. To make the notches, first drill 1"-diameter holes as shown in Fig. 1. Now cut up to the holes to complete the notches. Then round over the top and bottom edges of each notch and the front edges of the rail with a $1/4$" roundover bit.

I screwed the barrel rail in place through the back frame about two-thirds of the way up on the upper case; see Fig. 1a. (You may need to change the location of yours based on the length of your rifles.)

RIFLE BASE

The rifle base is cut from a piece of $3/4$"-thick edge-glued stock; see Fig. 1. Cut it to width and length to fit inside the upper case; see the photo on the opposite page and Fig. 1b.

After the rifle base is cut to size, lay out and cut the slots for the rifle butts; see Fig. 1. (Again, you may have to customize these to fit your rifles.) I rounded over the top edges of each slot and the front edge of the base piece with a $1/4$" roundover bit.

Finally, screw (don't glue) the base in place from the bottom of the upper case; see Fig. 1b.

SAFETY NOTE. I quite often add "Safety Notes" about using woodworking equipment. But here I would like to mention something else.

If you're going to build this gun cabinet, you should definitely add *secure* locks on both the upper and lower doors. Then keep both doors locked at all times and the keys safely away from children or anyone who should not be in the cabinet. Thanks.

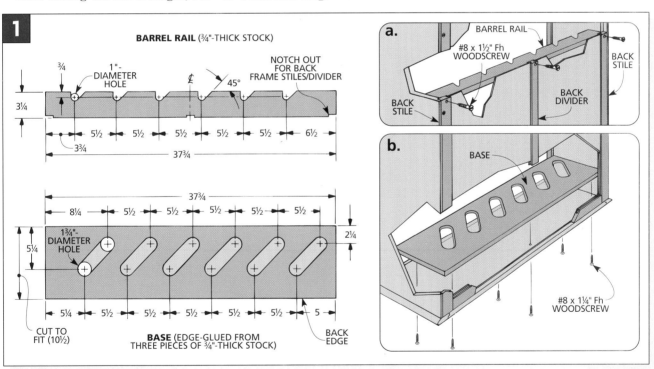

Locking the Cabinet

To help keep the guns and ammunition secure, I installed locks on the upper and lower right-hand doors; see photo. Each lock fits in a hole in the door rail, and hooks over a strike plate that's screwed to the back of the cabinet face rail; see cross section in drawing at right. With the right-hand doors locked, the left hand doors are locked securely in place by the astragals.

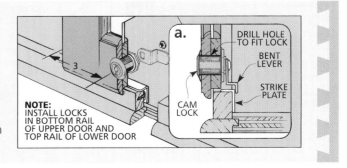

CHERRY ARMOIRE

The graceful arched top and raised-panel doors make this project an heirloom that will be handed down from generation to generation.

This armoire is the largest project featured in this book. But it's not the size, it's the details that really make it interesting.

ARCHED TOP. The most striking feature is the arched crown molding on the top of the cabinet — a detail that looks very difficult to build. Do you have to hand-carve the molding? Or use a shaper with a huge cutter?

Actually it's easier than it looks. It's done by building up and shaping pieces of 3/4"-thick stock with the help of a template, a router, and two common bits.

DETAILS. As with any project this size, there are lots of other details to work out. And it would be easy to be intimidated by all this work. But by conquering one detail at a time, it's not that difficult to complete this project.

WOOD. To build the armoire, I used a combination of solid cherry (for the doors, facing pieces, and base) and cherry plywood (for the case). There's a lot of it, and it's not exactly cheap. But keep in mind that this project will not only last your lifetime, but probably become a family heirloom.

FINISH. I finished the armoire with three coats of tung oil, hand-rubbing it in to bring out the beauty of the cherry.

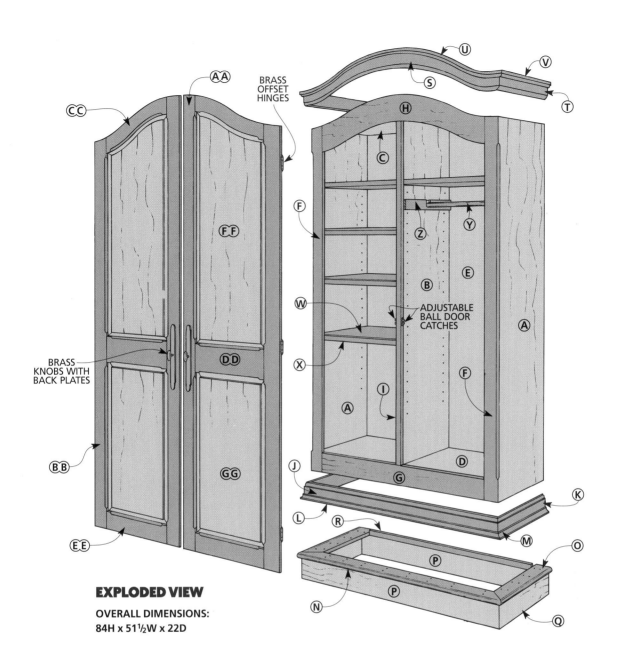

BRASS OFFSET HINGES

ADJUSTABLE BALL DOOR CATCHES

BRASS KNOBS WITH BACK PLATES

EXPLODED VIEW

OVERALL DIMENSIONS:
84H x 51½W x 22D

MATERIALS LIST

CASE

A	Sides (2)	¾ ply -19½ x 73
B	Divider (1)	¾ ply - 19¼ x 67¾
C	Top (1)	¾ ply - 46½ x 19
D	Bottom (1)	¾ ply - 46½ x 19¼
E	Back (1)	¼ ply - 47 x 73
F	Stiles (2)	¾ x 3 - 74 rough
G	Bottom Rail (1)	¾ x 4½ - 41½
H	Arched Top Rail (1)	¾ x 13½ rough- 41½
I	Divider Cap (1)	¾ x 1¼ - 69 rough
J	Ogee Frt. Mld. (1)	¾ x 2⅝ - 49
K	Ogee Side Mld. (2)	¾ x 2⅝ - 20¾
L	Cove Frt. Mld. (1)	⅝ x ⅝ - 50¼
M	Cove Side Mld. (2)	⅝ x ⅝ - 21⅜

BASE

N	Bullnose Front (1)	¾ x 2¾ - 51½
O	Bullnose Sides (2)	¾ x 2¾ - 22
P	Kickbd. Fr./Bk. (2)	¾ x 4¼ - 50½
Q	Kickbd. Sides (2)	¾ x 4¼ - 21½
R	Back Filler Strip (1)	¾ x 1¼ - 46

CROWN MOLDING

S	Base (Front) (1)	¾ x 3¼ - 51½ rough
T	Base (Sides) (2)	¾ x 3¼ - 22 rough
U	Trim (Front) (1)	¾ x 1¼ - 51½ rough
V	Trim (Sides) (2)	¾ x 1¼ - 22 rough

SHELVES AND ROD

W	Shelves (7)	¾ ply - 18½ x 22½
X	Shelf Edging (7)	¾ x 1 - 22½
Y	Clothes Rod (1)	1" dowel x 22⅛
Z	Rod Supports (2)	¾ x 2 - 19

DOORS

AA	Inside Stiles (2)	¾ x 3 - 68⅛
BB	Outside Stiles (2)	¾ x 3 - 64 rough
CC	Top (Arch) Rails (2)	¾ x 3 - 14⅝
DD	Middle Rails (2)	¾ x 4½ - 14⅝
EE	Bottom Rails (2)	¾ x 3 - 14⅝
FF	Top Panels (2)	¾ x 15¼ - 36 rough
GG	Bottom Panels (2)	¾ x 15¼ - 24⅜

HARDWARE SUPPLIES

(55) No. 6 x ⅝" Fh woodscrews
(22) No. 8 x 1¼" Fh woodscrews
(38) No. 8 x 1½" Fh woodscrews
(3 pr.) ⅜" Brass offset hinges
(2) Brass knobs with brass back plates
(2) Brass adjustable ball door catches
(28) Pin-type shelf supports
(4) ¼"-Dia. dowel pins, ¾" long

CUTTING DIAGRAM

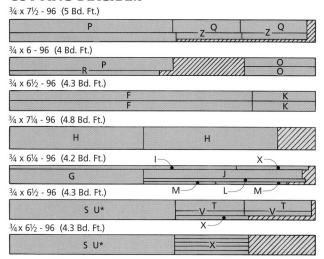

¾ x 7½ - 96 (5 Bd. Ft.)
| P | Z Q | Z Q |

¾ x 6 - 96 (4 Bd. Ft.)
| R — P | O / O |

¾ x 6½ - 96 (4.3 Bd. Ft.)
| F / F | K / K |

¾ x 7¼ - 96 (4.8 Bd. Ft.)
| H | H |

¾ x 6¼ - 96 (4.2 Bd. Ft.)
| G | I J X M L M |

¾ x 6½ - 96 (4.3 Bd. Ft.)
| S U* | V T V T X |

¾ x 6½ - 96 (4.3 Bd. Ft.)
| S U* | X |

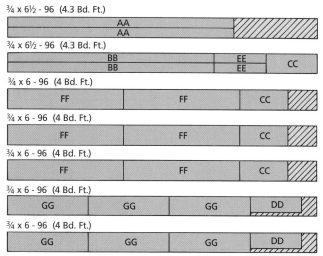

¾ x 6½ - 96 (4.3 Bd. Ft.)
| AA / AA | |

¾ x 6½ - 96 (4.3 Bd. Ft.)
| BB / BB | EE / EE | CC |

¾ x 6 - 96 (4 Bd. Ft.)
| FF | FF | CC |

¾ x 6 - 96 (4 Bd. Ft.)
| FF | FF | CC |

¾ x 6 - 96 (4 Bd. Ft.)
| FF | FF | CC |

¾ x 6 - 96 (4 Bd. Ft.)
| GG | GG | GG | DD |

¾ x 6 - 96 (4 Bd. Ft.)
| GG | GG | GG | DD |

*PARTS S, U ARE CUT FROM ONE GLUED-UP BLANK, SEE PAGE 85

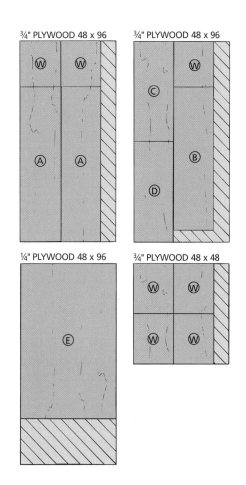

¾" PLYWOOD 48 x 96   (W, W, A, A)

¾" PLYWOOD 48 x 96   (W, C, B, D)

¼" PLYWOOD 48 x 96   (E)

¾" PLYWOOD 48 x 48   (W, W, W, W)

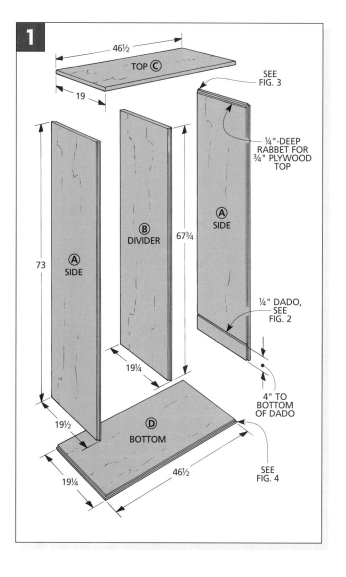

1

46½

TOP C

19

SEE FIG. 3

¼"-DEEP RABBET FOR ¾" PLYWOOD TOP

A SIDE

B DIVIDER

67¾

73

A SIDE

¼" DADO, SEE FIG. 2

4" TO BOTTOM OF DADO

19¼

19½

D BOTTOM

19¼

46½

SEE FIG. 4

CASE

I began building the armoire by cutting the parts for the case from $3/4$" plywood. Plywood is stable and not as likely to warp as solid stock so it's a good choice for the large pieces.

SIDES. Start by making the two side pieces (A); see Fig. 1. Although the sides are just two pieces of $3/4$" plywood, each side has a dado to accept the bottom (D) and a rabbet to accept the top (C) of the cabinet. These dadoes and rabbets must be perfectly aligned. The trick is to rout one dado and one rabbet across a *wide* blank of plywood. Then cut the blank in half to get two identical side pieces.

To make the sides (A), first cut a large blank to a finished length of 73" and rough width of 41"; see the plywood sheets shown on the Cutting Diagram on the opposite page.

DADO FOR BOTTOM. After cutting the blank to a finished length, I routed a dado across the blank to accept the bottom piece (D); see Fig. 2. To rout the dado, clamp a straightedge fence across the blank so a $1/4$" straight bit in the router will be positioned 4" up from the bottom end; see Fig. 1.

RABBET FOR TOP. After routing the dado, the next step is to rout a $1/4$"-deep rabbet along the top end of the blank (on the same face as the dado) to accept the top piece (C); see Fig. 3. I did this by mounting an edge guide and a $1/2$" straight bit in the router, and then making two passes.

CUT CASE SIDES. Now, to get the two case sides (A), I ripped the plywood blank into two $19^1/2$"-wide pieces.

BACK RABBET. After the side pieces are cut apart, rout a $1/4$" x $1/2$" rabbet on the *back* edge of each piece to attach the case back; see Fig. 3. (Note: Be sure to cut the back rabbet so you will end up with a mirrored set of side pieces.)

DIVIDER. Next, cut a divider (B) from $3/4$" plywood; see Fig. 1. Since the cabinet back fits behind it, cut the divider $1/4$" less in width than the side pieces. (This meant I cut my divider $19^1/4$" wide.)

To determine the length of the divider, measure the distance between the dado and the rabbet on the side pieces (68") and subtract $1/4$" (to allow for the tongue that will be cut on the ends of the bottom piece). (In my case, I cut the divider $67^3/4$" long.)

TOP AND BOTTOM. The last pieces of $3/4$" plywood to cut for the case are the top (C) and bottom (D); see Fig. 1. To determine the width of the top piece (C), measure the side pieces and subtract $1/2$". (In my case this made the top piece 19" wide.)

The bottom piece (D) has a $1/4$" tongue on the front edge to later accept a hardwood facing rail, so cut it $1/4$" wider ($19^1/4$") than the top piece. After the top and bottom pieces are cut to width, cut both pieces to a uniform length of $46^1/2$".

TONGUES. The final step before assembly is to cut $1/4$"-thick tongues on the front edges of the side pieces (A), divider (B), and bottom piece (D); see Fig. 4. These tongues are used to attach hardwood facing; refer to Fig. 6 on page 82. At the same time, cut identical tongues on the ends of the bottom piece (D) to fit into the dadoes in the side pieces (A).

To make the tongues, rout $1/4$"-wide rabbets on the top and bottom edges with a router bit and edge guide. Sneak up on the final fit by increasing the depth of cut until the tongue between the rabbets just fits into the dadoes in the side pieces.

CASE ASSEMBLY

After all the tongues are formed, the case can be assembled; see Fig. 5. Start by standing the divider (B) on its front edge (with the tongue facing down) and screwing and gluing it between the top (C) and the bottom (D). I used No. 8 x $1^1/2$" flathead woodscrews.

Next, add the side pieces (A). Glue the tongue on the bottom into the dado in the sides; see Fig. 5a. Then screw the side pieces into the top (C). (These

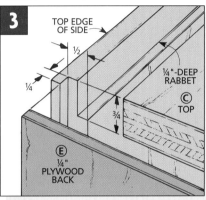

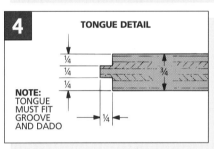

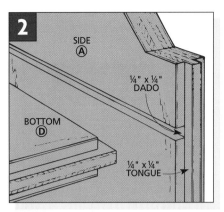

screws will be covered later by a molding strip.)

BACK PANEL. To square up the case, I cut a plywood back (E) from $1/4$" cherry plywood to fit between the rabbets in the side panels; see Fig. 3. Then screw it to the case; see Fig. 5.

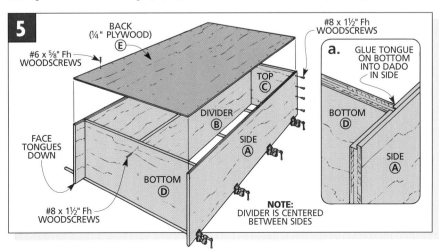

FACE FRAME

Now that the plywood case is assembled, the front edges can be faced.

STILES. Start by cutting two stiles (F) $3^1/_{16}$" wide and 1" longer than the side pieces. (Note: After assembly, the stiles are trimmed flush with the side of the case and to length; see Fig. 8a.)

Next, cut a groove on the inside face of each stile to fit over the tongue on the side (A); see Fig. 7. Position the tongue $5/_{16}$" from the edge of the stile. (This leaves a $1/_{16}$" overhang for trimming.)

After cutting the grooves, rout a $1/_4$"-wide mortise centered on the inside edge of each stile at the top; see Fig. 8. This mortise will accept a spline to join the stile to the arched top rail (H). (Note: I cut the mortises with the mortising table shown on pages 92–93.)

Before you can glue on the stiles, you have to trim back $2^1/_4$" of the tongue on the front of the bottom (D); see Fig. 6.

BOTTOM RAIL. With the stiles glued on, measure between them to determine the length of the bottom rail (G). Then cut the rail to this length and $4^9/_{16}$" wide. (It's trimmed to $4^1/_2$" later.)

Next, cut a groove in the rail to fit over the tongue on the bottom (D). (This groove is like the one on the stile; see Fig. 7.) Then glue the rail in place.

TOP RAIL. The most difficult piece to make is the arched top rail (H). To make the job easier, I made a template. This template will also be used later to make the moldings that are glued on top of the rail.

TEMPLATE. I made the template out of $1/_4$"-thick hardboard. Begin by cutting the hardboard $13^1/_2$" wide and $51^1/_2$" long; see Step 1 in Fig. 9. This makes the template long enough to use on both molding pieces (S, U) as well as the top rail (H).

The template can become a "story stick" by laying out reference lines with measurements taken from the cabinet.

To do this, first mark a centerline on the length of the template blank; see Step 1. Then mark vertical reference

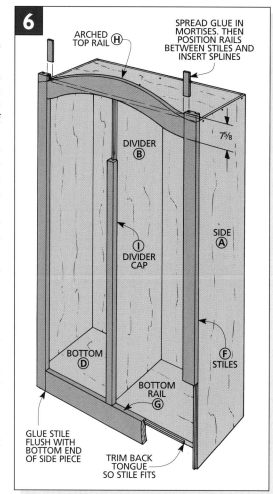

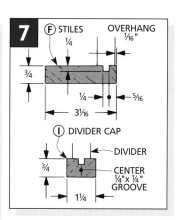

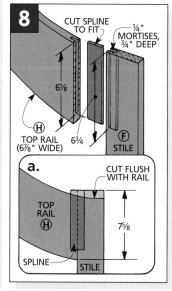

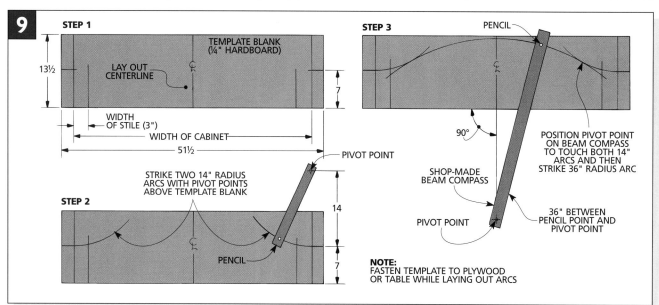

lines at both ends to indicate the width of the cabinet (47½" in my case).

Next, mark a second set of vertical lines to indicate the door openings. To determine this measurement, I measured in from the first set of lines the final width of the stiles (3").

Finally, mark horizontal lines at both ends 7" up from the bottom.

Now the arched curve can be laid out by drawing three arcs using shop-built beam compasses. I made these compasses from strips of hardboard.

First, two small arcs are laid out from above the left and right corners of the template; see Step 2. Then a large connecting arc is laid out from below the bottom edge of the template; see Step 3.

Next, cut the arched top of the template a little oversize with a sabre saw or band saw and sand right up to the line.

RAIL BLANK. Now you can use the template to make the top rail (H) of the armoire. Begin by edge-gluing a 13½"-wide blank from ¾" stock to fit between the cabinet stiles (41½" long in my case); see Fig. 10. Then mark a centerline on the blank.

CUT OUT ARCH. After the centerline is marked, lay the template on top of the blank and align the bottom edges and centerlines; see Fig. 10. Then draw the outline of the arch on the blank.

Next remove the template and cut out the shape, staying about ⅛" outside the pencil line; see Fig. 10a.

FLUSH TRIM SMOOTH. Now, here's the trick for making the top rail the exact same shape as the template.

First, screw the template to the blank, aligning the bottom edges and centerlines; see Fig. 11. (Note: The screw holes will be covered later by moldings if you position them 1¾" down from the arched edge.)

Next, turn the blank and template upside down and clamp them down to your bench; see Fig. 12. Then mount a flush trim bit in your router and lower the bit so the bearing rides against the template; see Fig. 12a.

Now when you run the bearing along the template, the bit will trim the edge the same shape as the template.

CUT OFF BOTTOM. With the top edge cut, the bottom edge of the rail can be cut parallel to the top. Even though the edges are parallel, the radius for the bottom edge is different from the top, so you can't use the same template.

To mark the bottom edge, I used a scribing stick. This scribing stick is just an 8"-long piece of hardboard with two nails driven in at one end; see Fig. 13a.

Now, with both nails riding along the top of the arch, scribe the bottom edge on the blank; see Fig. 13. Then cut it slightly oversize and sand up to the line.

ROUT MORTISES. After the rail was cut to shape, I routed mortises on both ends to match the ones in the stiles; see Fig. 8. Then brush glue into all the mortises and fit the top rail between the stiles. Finally, slide splines into the mortises from the open top end; see Fig. 6.

Once the glue dries, extend the curve from the top onto the stiles, and cut it off with a sabre saw; see Fig. 8a.

DIVIDER CAP. The last facing piece is the divider cap (I). It's cut 1¼" wide and to length to fit between the top and bottom rails; see Fig. 6. Then cut a groove on the inside of the cap to fit over the tongue on the divider; see Fig. 7.

TRIM FACING FLUSH. After the cap is glued on, you can trim the stiles (F) flush with the outside of the side pieces, and the bottom rail (G) flush with the top of the bottom piece. To do this I used a router and flush trim bit. (Note: On the top of the bottom rail, the bit won't cut square into the inside corners. So I cleaned these up with a chisel.)

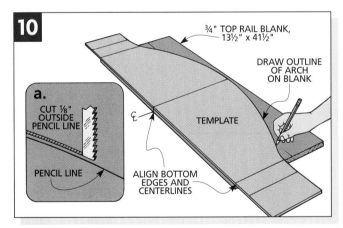

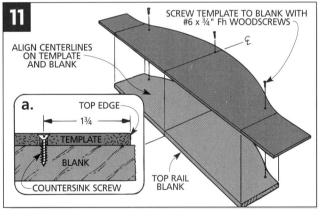

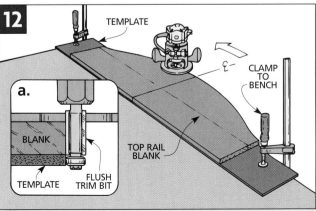

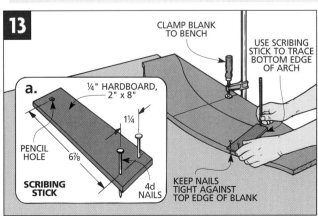

BASE

After adding the face frame to the case, I began work on the base. The base is a bullnose frame glued on top of a kickboard frame; see Fig. 14.

TOP FRAME. To make the bullnose frame, rip a front (N) and two sides (O) to a width of $2^3/4$"; see Fig. 14. Then rough cut the front 53" long and the sides 23" long.

Before cutting the pieces to final length, use the router table to rout a bullnose edge on the pieces. First, rout a $1/2$" roundover on the top edge; see Step 1 in Fig. 15. Then, rout a $1/4$" roundover on the bottom edge; see Step 2.

After the pieces are routed, miter both ends of the front piece (N) 4" longer ($51^1/2$") than the width of the plywood case. Then miter the front end of each side piece (O) and cut the back end square so it's 2" longer (22") than the depth of the plywood case.

Before gluing the bullnose pieces together, I drilled a series of countersunk screw holes through them; see Fig. 14a. These screws are used to mount the bullnose frame down to the kickboard frame and up to the bottom of the plywood cabinet; see Fig. 16a.

Now glue the miters together to form the three-sided frame. (Just hold the pieces until the glue sets.)

KICKBOARD. The rest of the base consists of a kickboard front, back (both P) and two sides (Q). Rip these pieces to a width of $4^1/4$"; see Fig. 14.

Then miter both ends of the kickboard front and back pieces (P) so the length of each is 1" shorter than the bullnose frame ($50^1/2$"). Next, miter both ends of each side (Q) so the length is $1/2$" shorter than the bullnose frame sides ($21^1/2$").

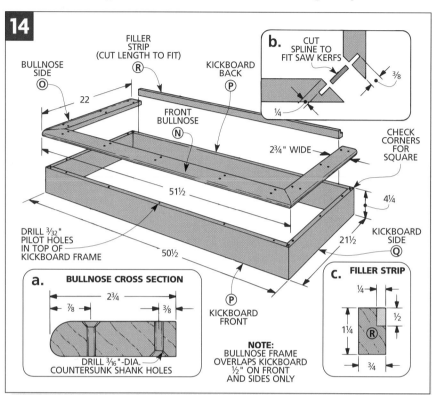

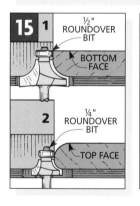

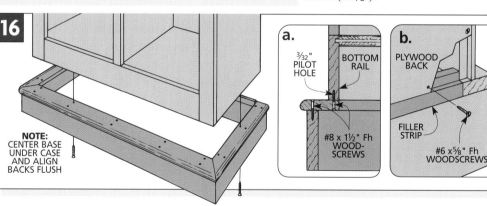

Burnishing a Miter

As I was building the armoire, I ran into a problem at one corner of the base — the miter joint had a slight gap in it.

Should I start over and cut new pieces to make it perfect? Or is there an easy way to fix it?

There's a neat little trick for closing outside miters that's used on base moldings in houses. You just "burnish" the corners to close the gap.

When the gap on an outside miter is $1/16$" or less you can roll both sides of the

joint over to fill the gap. To burnish the miter on the base, I used a screwdriver.

Hold the screwdriver at a very slight angle to the workpiece. Then press down hard to bend the fibers slightly as you stroke down the joint.

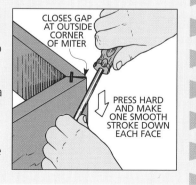

KERF AND SPLINE. To help keep the miters aligned, I cut a kerf in each miter; see Fig. 14b. Then I cut a spline to fit the kerfs.

BASE ASSEMBLY. Now the kickboard frame can be glued together. Then glue and screw the bullnose frame to the top of the kickboard frame; see Fig. 14.

FILLER STRIP. One final step on the base is to cut a filler strip (R) to fit on top of the kickboard back; see Fig. 14c. Before gluing the filler strip in place, cut a rabbet along the top edge of the strip to accept the cabinet back; see Fig. 16b.

BASE TO CASE. After the base is complete, it can be attached to the case; see Fig. 16. To do this, I laid the case down on its back.

Now center the base on the case and align it flush across the back of the case; see Fig. 16b. When they're in position, drill pilot holes through the shank holes in the bullnose frame and into the bottom of the case; see Fig. 16a. Then screw them together and the back to the filler strip; see Fig. 16b.

ARCHED MOLDING

On the armoire, the arched top rail (explained on pages 82–83) serves as a foundation for arched molding. The molding itself is made from two pieces glued together — a base piece (S) with a Roman ogee and a trim piece (U) with a roundover; refer to Fig. 21 on page 86.

CUT FROM ONE BLANK. Both pieces can be laid out and cut from one large edge-glued blank; see Fig. 17. After the glue dries, draw a vertical centerline on the blank.

TOP EDGE. The process for cutting the top edge of each piece is exactly the same as on the top rail. I used the same template as with the top rail and marked and cut the top edge slightly oversize; refer back to Fig. 10. Next screw the template to the blank (Fig. 11) and trim the piece flush (Fig. 12).

BOTTOM EDGE. To cut the bottom edge, you could use the same process as on the top rail. But I tried something a little different here. Since both pieces are narrower, I used the band saw to get a more uniform cut.

To do this, clamp a pointed guide block to the band saw table so the distance between the blade and the block is about $1/16''$ wider than the finished width of the molding; see Fig. 18. (The $1/16''$ will be sanded off later.) For the

base molding (S), clamp the block $3^5/_{16}''$ from the blade.

Now cut the bottom edge of the molding by running the top (routed) edge against the guide block.

SECOND MOLDING. After cutting the base strip (S), you can follow the whole procedure over again for the trim strip (U). When cutting this piece, clamp the guide block $1^5/_{16}''$ from the blade.

SAND TO WIDTH. At this point, each molding piece should be fairly uniform in width, but about $1/16''$ oversize and have a rough bottom edge from the band saw cut. I smoothed the bottom edge with a sanding drum on the drill press; see Fig. 19.

To do this, clamp a curved (convex) guide block to the drill press table and feed the molding strip between the block and the sanding drum. The convex curve on the guide block should match the concave curve on the top edge of the molding. (Shop Note: I used

a convex section of the waste left over from cutting the strips from the blank.)

Clamp the guide block so the sanding drum will sand the molding strip very lightly. Then feed the strip with a steady movement from left to right. (Don't stop or you'll get a divot in the molding strip.)

Take a couple of passes at each setting, then move the guide block slightly closer to the sanding drum and repeat the procedure. Once the bottom edge is smooth and the strip is the correct width ($3^1/_4''$ or $1^1/_4''$), stop sanding.

ROUT PROFILES. Before gluing the moldings together, I routed profiles along the bottom edges; see Fig. 20.

For the base strip (S), I used a Roman ogee bit along the bottom edge. To prevent chipout, rout in a series of passes until there's a $1/8''$ shoulder at the bottom of the cut; see Fig 20a.

On the trim strip (U), I routed a roundover with a shoulder; see Fig. 20a.

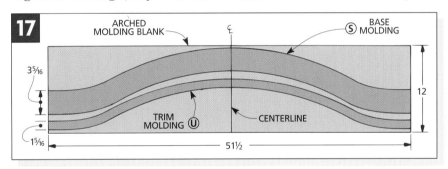

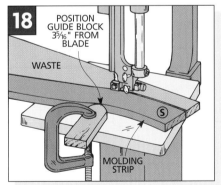

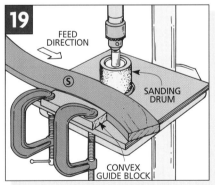

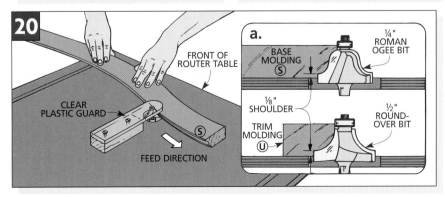

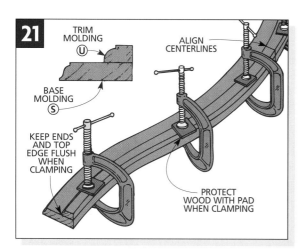

21

TRIM MOLDING Ⓤ

ALIGN CENTERLINES

BASE MOLDING Ⓢ

KEEP ENDS AND TOP EDGE FLUSH WHEN CLAMPING

PROTECT WOOD WITH PAD WHEN CLAMPING

ASSEMBLE ARCHED MOLDINGS

After the profiles are routed on the arched molding pieces, the pieces can be glued together. The trick here is to make sure that the top edges and ends align. I found that the easiest way to do this was to align the centerlines that I had previously marked on both pieces; see Fig. 21. Then when gluing use enough clamps to keep consistent pressure on both of the pieces; see the photo on the next page.

MITERING THE ENDS

Once you've glued the two arched molding strips together you're faced with another interesting challenge. How do you cut clean, straight miters on the ends of a piece that's $1\frac{1}{2}$" thick, $51\frac{1}{2}$" long, and shaped like a boa constrictor?

And, if that's not enough of a problem, the two miters have to be the correct distance apart or the molding won't fit the cabinet.

MITERING CARRIAGE. To solve all of this, I approached the last problem first. I figured if I could cut miters the correct distance apart on the ends of a *straight* board, I could transfer this measurement to the arched molding. That led to the idea of using a simple carriage (cut to the correct length) to hold the arched molding while cutting the miters on both ends.

CARRIAGE BASE. To make the carriage, start by cutting a base from a piece of $\frac{1}{4}$" plywood or hardboard. I cut the base to a width of 11" and 48" long; see Fig. 22.

FENCES. Then screw $\frac{3}{4}$"-thick fences on top of the panel along the front and back edges; see Fig 22a. Keep the screws at least 2" from each end so you won't hit them when cutting the carriage to length.

MITER ONE END. Next, clamp your table saw miter gauge to the back fence near one end of the carriage and set the carriage on top of the saw; see Fig. 23. Then tip your saw blade to 45° and trim just a little bit off one end of the carriage. (Don't cut the molding yet, just cut the carriage for now.)

Shop Note: You can also use this carriage on a radial arm saw without a miter gauge. Just tip the blade to 45° and hold the carriage tight against the fence when cutting.

MITER TO LENGTH. The trick comes in cutting the miter on the other end of the carriage to the correct length. To determine the finished length of the molding, measure the outside width of the cabinet. (In my case, $47\frac{1}{2}$".)

Then, to cut the carriage to this

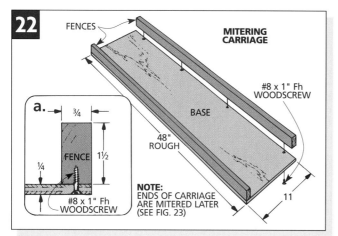

22

FENCES

MITERING CARRIAGE

#8 x 1" Fh WOODSCREW

BASE

48" ROUGH

a. $\frac{3}{4}$

FENCE $1\frac{1}{2}$

$\frac{1}{4}$

#8 x 1" Fh WOODSCREW

NOTE: ENDS OF CARRIAGE ARE MITERED LATER (SEE FIG. 23)

11

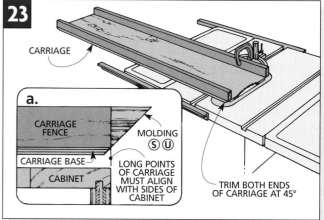

23

CARRIAGE

a.

CARRIAGE FENCE

MOLDING Ⓢ Ⓤ

CARRIAGE BASE

CABINET

LONG POINTS OF CARRIAGE MUST ALIGN WITH SIDES OF CABINET

TRIM BOTH ENDS OF CARRIAGE AT 45°

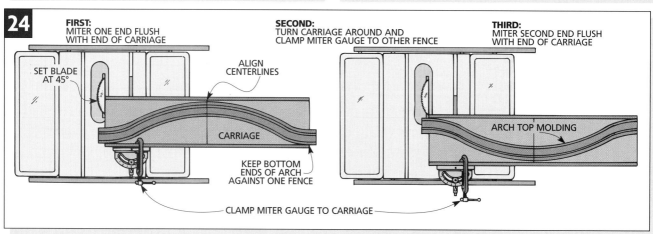

24

FIRST: MITER ONE END FLUSH WITH END OF CARRIAGE

SECOND: TURN CARRIAGE AROUND AND CLAMP MITER GAUGE TO OTHER FENCE

THIRD: MITER SECOND END FLUSH WITH END OF CARRIAGE

SET BLADE AT 45°

ALIGN CENTERLINES

CARRIAGE

KEEP BOTTOM ENDS OF ARCH AGAINST ONE FENCE

ARCH TOP MOLDING

CLAMP MITER GAUGE TO CARRIAGE

length, I unclamped the miter gauge and turned the carriage around so the other fence is against the miter gauge. Next, make a series of cuts sneaking up on the final dimension until the distance from *long point-to-long point* of the miters measures the same as the outside width of the cabinet; see Fig. 23a.

Wait a minute. I thought you said you were going to cut the carriage the same length as the finished arched molding. To fit the cabinet, wouldn't that be from *short point-to-short point* of the miters?

This may seem a little confusing. But remember, you're going to be setting the molding on *top* of the carriage for cutting. So the long points on the top of the carriage base will actually become the short points on the back of the molding; see Fig. 23a.

MOUNT THE WORKPIECE. Once the carriage is cut to the correct length, draw a line across it centered on the length; see Fig. 24. Then you can mount the molding on top of the carriage.

To cut an even amount off both ends, align the centerlines on the molding with the centerline on the carriage; see Fig. 24. And keep both "feet" of the arch (low points) tight against one of the fences. (I used double-sided carpet tape to hold the molding in place, but you could screw up from the bottom of the carriage into the back of the molding.)

MITER ONE END. After the molding is in position, clamp the miter gauge to the back fence so the saw blade aligns with the miter cut on the end of the carriage; see Fig. 24. Then trim one end off the molding at a 45° angle.

CUT TO LENGTH. Next, turn the carriage completely around and clamp the miter gauge to the other fence so the blade aligns with the miter on the other end. Then cut the molding to the finished length. Now the short points on the molding should just fit the outside edges of the cabinet.

SCREW IN PLACE. After the arched molding is cut to fit the cabinet, it can be screwed to the front of the top rail (H); see Fig. 25a.

OTHER MOLDINGS

Now there are a few more moldings to add to the top and bottom of the cabinet.

SIDE CROWN MOLDING. First there are two side crown molding strips (T,V) that have the same profiles as the arched front molding; see Fig. 25b.

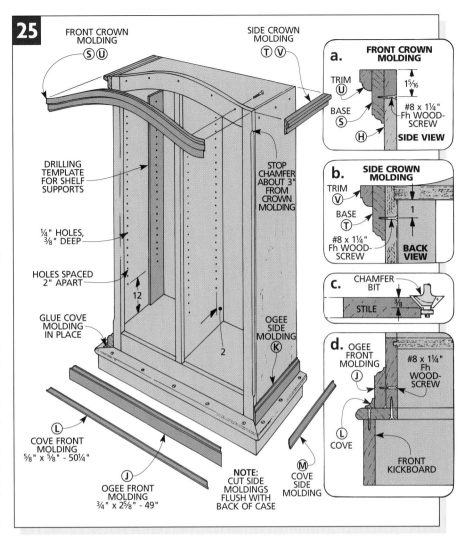

After the pieces are routed and glued together, miter the front ends and cut the back ends off square with the back of the cabinet; see Fig. 25. Then screw the side moldings to the side of the cabinet from inside; see Fig. 25b.

BASE MOLDING. The next molding to be added is around the base of the cabinet; see Fig. 25. To make the ogee moldings (J, K), cut enough $2\frac{5}{8}$"-wide stock to fit around the front and sides of the cabinet. Then rout a Roman ogee on the top edge of each piece. Miter a front piece (J) to fit across the front of the cabinet and screw it in place from behind; see Fig. 25d.

Now, miter the front ends of the side pieces (K), and then cut off the back ends flush with the back of the case. Screw these pieces in place as well.

Next, add cove molding (L, M) in front of the ogee molding. To make these strips, rout a $\frac{1}{2}$" cove on the edges of a $1\frac{1}{2}$"-wide strip of $\frac{5}{8}$"-thick stock. Then trim the $\frac{5}{8}$"-wide molding

off the outside edges. Now miter the molding to fit around the case and glue the strips in place.

CHAMFER. After all the molding was attached, I added another little detail to the case. I routed $\frac{3}{8}$" stopped chamfers on the front corners of the case starting and stopping 3" from the molding at the top and the base; see Figs. 25 and 25c.

SHELF SUPPORT HOLES

It's easiest to drill holes for pin-type shelf supports on the inside of the cabinet now — *before* you add the doors. The supports fit into $\frac{1}{4}$" holes drilled $\frac{3}{8}$" deep into the cabinet sides (A) and center divider (B); see Fig. 25.

DRILLING TEMPLATE. To help position the holes consistently, I made a template from a 4"-wide piece of $\frac{1}{4}$" hardboard. Then, to drill the holes, hold the template tight down on the cabinet bottom and drill through the pre-drilled holes in the template; see Fig. 25.

DOOR FRAMES

After the basic cabinet is complete, work can begin on the doors.

STILES. Begin by cutting all the stiles 3" wide and the two outside stiles (BB) to a rough length of 64"; see Fig. 26.

To determine the length of the inside stiles (AA), measure the height of the door openings at their highest point ($67^5/8$" in my case.) Then, since the doors overlap the case by $1/4$", add $1/2$".

RAILS. Next, I cut the rails. First, glue-up two 9"-wide blanks for the top rails (CC); see Fig. 27. (The arch shape will be cut later.) Then rip the middle rails (DD) $4^1/2$" wide and the bottom rails (EE) 3" wide; see Fig. 28.

To determine their lengths, measure across the door opening ($20^1/8$") and subtract the combined width of the two stiles (6"). Then add $1/2$" for the overlap.

MORTISES. I assembled the frames with mortise and spline joints; see pages 91 – 94. (You could use a biscuit joiner as well.) Start by laying out the locations of the mortises on all the rails; see Figs. 27 and 28.

To transfer the locations of the mortises to the stiles (see Fig. 29), I laid all of the pieces down as they would appear in the assembled door; see Fig. 26. Then, mark and cut the mortises in both the stiles and rails. (Note: The $1/4$"-wide mortises are offset on the thickness to align with grooves cut later.)

Now, cut splines to fit the mortises and dry assemble the door frames.

CUTTING THE ARCH. The next step is to cut the top door rails (CC) to their arched shape. To do this I made a cardboard template by tracing the arched door opening; see Fig. 30. Then cut out the template and transfer the shape to the rail and outside stile; see Fig. 31.

After cutting the top edge of the rails and top end of the outside stiles to shape, cut the bottom edge of the arched rails using the band saw and sander technique shown on page 85.

PANEL GROOVES. The last step on the door frames is to rout grooves around the inside of the stiles and rails for the raised panels; see Fig. 32. I cut the grooves with a $1/4$" slot cutter on the router table.

To do this, raise the bit until it's aligned with the mortises. Then, rout the grooves along the inside edges of the rails. On the stiles, don't rout beyond the mortises; see Fig. 32a.

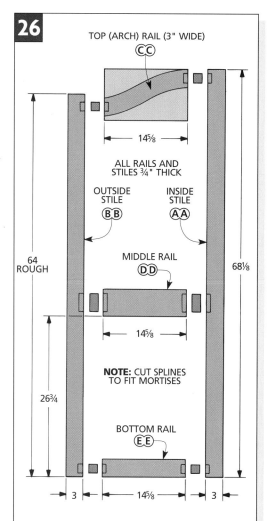

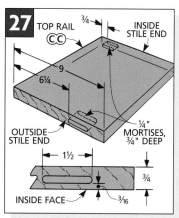

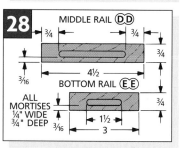

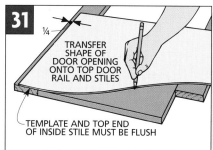

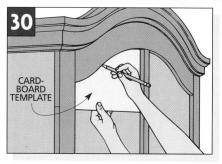

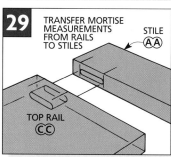

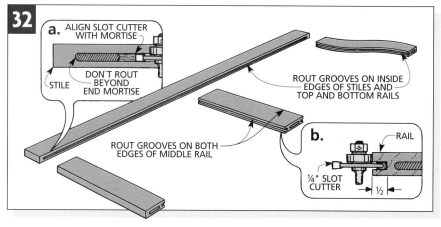

DOOR PANELS

Next, I dry assembled the frames and routed stopped chamfers around the inside of each frame; see Figs. 33 and 34.

Shop Note: If you place a $3/4$"-wide block in each corner, the bearing will hit the block and stop the chamfer $5/8$" from the inside corner.

PANELS. Now work can begin on the raised panels. Start by edge-gluing enough $3/4$"-thick stock to make two top panel (FF) blanks and two bottom panel (GG) blanks. To determine the finished size of the panels, measure the frame openings and add $5/8$" to the height and width to allow for tongues on the panels. After you know the size of the panels, cut the bottom panels to size.

To lay out each top panel (FF), center the panel on the opening and trace the arch onto the panel. Then cut along the curved line. To determine where to cut the bottom edge, measure the height of the opening and add $5/8$" for the tongues.

RAISING THE PANELS. I routed the bevel for the raised panel with a $1\,7/16$"-dia. raised panel bit (Sears bit No. 25465 or similar) and the router table; see Fig. 35 and box below.

RABBET. Next, turn the panels over and rout a rabbet in the back; see Step 3 in Fig. 35. Note: The panel is cut to fit only $5/16$" into the slot, but a $3/8$" rabbet is cut in it. This allows a $1/16$" gap for the panel to expand with changes in humidity.

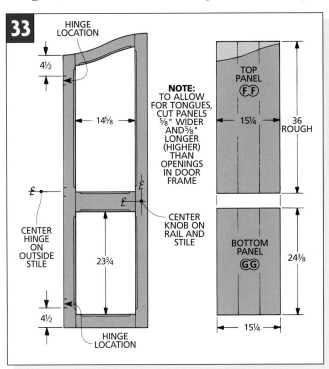

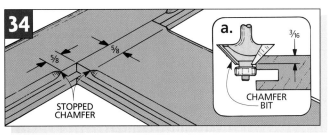

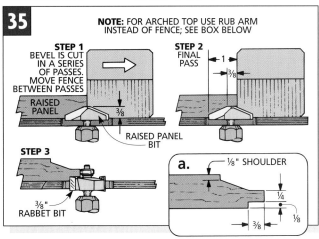

Rub Arm for Raised Panels

Cutting profiles on arched raised panels is usually done with shaper cutters or expensive router bits. These bits have bearings that follow the shape of the arch.

However, on the armoire I tried a less expensive bit that doesn't have a bearing.

For the straight sections of the panels, I used the router table fence.

But for the arched top edge I added a rub arm positioned over the top of the bit; see Fig. 1.

To rout the beveled edge, draw a reference line on top

of the rub arm. Then, to maintain a consistent width on the profile, move the workpiece so the edge is perpendicular to that line; see Fig. 2.

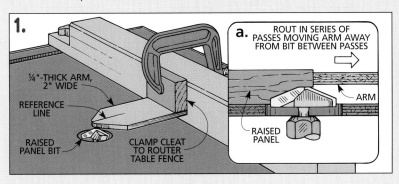

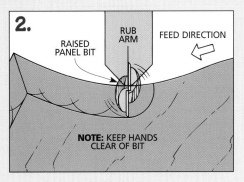

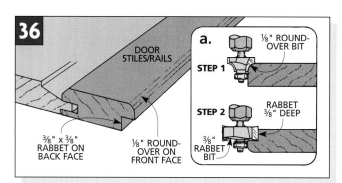

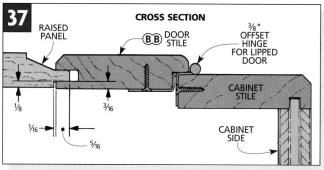

DOOR ASSEMBLY

Now the doors can be assembled. Glue up the mortise and spline joints, but don't put any glue on the panels or in the slots. (The panel has to be able to expand and contract; see box below.)

ROUNDOVER AND RABBET. There are two more steps on the doors. Round over the front edges; see Step 1 in Fig. 36a. Then rout a rabbet in the back edges; see Step 2.

HARDWARE. Now the doors can be mounted with offset hinges; see Fig. 37. Position the hinges $4\frac{1}{2}$" from the top and bottom of the door and centered on the height of the stile; refer to Fig. 33.

Finally, screw the knobs, decorative backing plates, and door catches to the inside door stiles; see the Exploded View on page 79 and Fig. 33. The catches should align with the knobs.

SHELVES

The last step is to make the shelves and add a clothes rod if you want.

CUT TO SIZE. To determine the size of the shelves (W), measure the inside of the case. But to allow for edging on the front of the shelves, I cut the shelves $\frac{1}{2}$" *less* in width than the depth of my case. Then cut them to length $\frac{1}{8}$" less than the distance between the divider and the cabinet side.

EDGING. After cutting the shelves to size, the next step is to rout tongues on the front for the edging; see Fig. 38.

Now cut the 1"-wide shelf edging (X) from $\frac{3}{4}$"-thick stock. Next cut grooves off-center on each strip to fit over the tongues on the shelves. And then glue the edging in place; see Fig. 38.

CLOTHES ROD. If you want to use the armoire to hang clothes, you will have to add a rod (Y); see Fig. 39. I supported the rod with two supports (Z). The supports are held in place with two pins that fit into the shelf support holes.

Cut the supports from $\frac{3}{4}$"-thick stock and drill 1" holes, only $\frac{1}{2}$" deep centered on each piece. Then rout an "escape" area for the rod to be removed above one of the holes; see Fig. 15a.

Now drill holes and mount $\frac{1}{4}$" dowel pins on the back side of each support to align with the holes in the cabinet. Finally, cut a 1"-dia. dowel to length so it wedges between the supports. ■

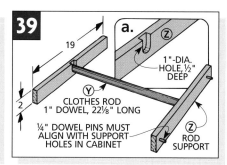

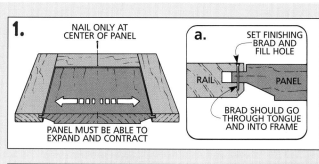

Floating Panels

When assembling a solid wood panel into a frame, the panel must be free to expand and contract with seasonal changes in humidity. That's why you shouldn't glue the panel into the frame.

Okay, but if the panel is free to move, what keeps it centered in the frame?

One solution is to turn the frame over and pin the panel with brads; see Fig. 1. Before nailing, check that the panel is centered in the frame. Then drive a

single brad centered at the top and bottom of each panel. The brad should go through the tongue and into the rail; see Fig. 1a.

A second method is to use foam rubber in the slots; see Fig. 2. Putting foam rubber on all four sides of the panel keeps it centered, and when the panel expands, the foam compresses.

I've found $\frac{1}{4}$"-wide foam weatherstripping tape with an adhesive back fits perfectly in the $\frac{1}{4}$" groove.

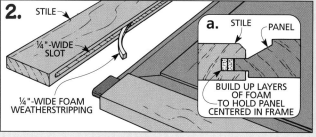

Typically, when I have to build a frame and panel, the joint I would choose first is the traditional mortise and tenon joint. Although mortise and tenon joints could be used for the frames on the armoire shown on page 78 — I didn't.

Instead, I used a "hybrid" joint, a mortise and *spline*. It consists of two mortises joined by a connecting piece called a spline; see drawing at right.

ADVANTAGES. There are a couple of advantages to using this joint instead of a mortise and tenon.

First, if you're building a project with angled rails or legs, angled tenons are required. These are not only difficult to cut, but they're also difficult to fit.

But there's another reason. When cutting a tenon on the end of a large piece like the arched top rail of the armoire, the operation can be awkward, and dangerous on a table saw.

QUESTIONS. Okay, once I decided to use a mortise and spline joint, there were some questions to ask. How large should the mortise be? And what's the best material to use for splines?

SIZE OF MORTISE. As a rule of thumb, mortises are usually one third the thickness of the stock to be joined. For example, when working with ³/₄"-thick stock, I cut ¹/₄"-wide mortises.

SPLINES. As for the splines, I use either ¹/₄"-thick plywood or hardboard. Both of these materials are ideal

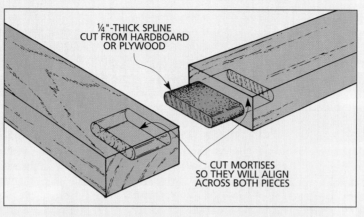

¹/₄"-THICK SPLINE CUT FROM HARDBOARD OR PLYWOOD

CUT MORTISES SO THEY WILL ALIGN ACROSS BOTH PIECES

because they are slightly less than ¹/₄"-thick — which means they fit in the mortises easily, with room for a good glue surface.

My preference is to use hardboard. It cuts a little cleaner than plywood and the edges are easier to round over to match the mortises. (I use tempered hardboard — the kind that's smooth on both sides.)

DOWELS. Wouldn't it be easier to drill holes and use dowels?

I've never been very fond of dowels. First, it's difficult to drill holes in opposing pieces so that they align accurately. Second, as dowels dry they tend to "oval-out" in the round hole providing a weak joint. And, finally, dowels don't provide as much glue surface as a spline; see photos below.

BISCUIT JOINERS. What about using a biscuit joiner?

Biscuit joiners work great on some projects. But there's one big drawback. You can't use them to join a frame if the rails are narrower than 1³/₄" wide — the biscuits are too long to fit in the end of

the rail. (Note: An exception to this is the Ryobi Detail Biscuit Joiner that cuts very small mortises for miniature biscuits.)

With a mortise and spline joint you can make the mortise and the spline whatever size you need for your project.

One other advantage is that the glue surface provided by a spline is larger than that of a biscuit; see the photos below.

MORTISE AND SPLINE. As you can probably tell, I'm excited about this joint. You can cut the mortises on a drill press, but I've found it easier to cut them on the shop-built mortising table shown on pages 92 and 93. With this table I can cut clean, accurate mortises and add a spline — all in a fraction of the time it used to take to cut mortise and tenon joints.

BITS. The whole idea of the mortising table is to cut mortises with a router that's mounted horizontally. To do this you can use a regular straight bit (like a two-flute carbide-tipped straight bit). However, I would highly recommend using a spiral end mill bit. These bits are specifically designed to make plunge cuts and rout side-to-side much easier than straight bits.

STEP-BY-STEP. Once you have the mortising table and the bits, it's a simple matter to cut the mortises. You'll find step-by-step instructions on page 94 for cutting the mortises and making the splines.

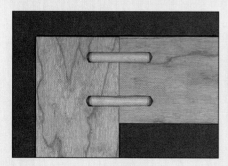

DOWELS

Of all the joints shown, this is the most familiar. However, alignment can be difficult and there's very little glue surface.

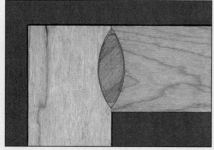

BISCUIT JOINT

This relatively new joint is easy to make, but it requires a special machine. And the size of the biscuits limits their use.

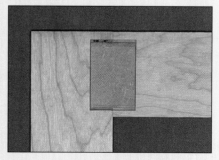

MORTISE AND SPLINE

The connecting spline of this joint provides a large gluing surface. Plus the size can be varied to fit many applications.

Mortising Table . . . . *Shop Jig*

This table for mortising is basically a plywood box with a high back panel. Then a router is mounted to the back so the router bit sticks through to cut a mortise.

It's a simple idea that solves the problems often involved with cutting mortises on a router table or drill press. First, the workpiece lays flat, rather than on edge. Second, the mortise can be cut to full depth in a series of passes without having to change the position of the bit. (For more on using the table; see page 94.)

BASE FRAME

To make the base frame, start by cutting the top (A) and bottom (B) 11½" wide and 15¾" long out of ¾" plywood; see Fig. 1.

After cutting the top and bottom, cut two sides (C) 4¼" wide by 11½" long. Then I cut a 11¼"-long center divider (D) to form an enclosed box so I could use a shop vacuum to remove chips; see Fig. 1.

SHOP VACUUM. If you're using a shop vacuum, cut a hole in one of the side pieces (C) to accept the end of the hose. If you're not going to use a vacuum, leave out the center divider so you can clean out the sawdust by hand.

DADOES. After the base pieces are cut to size, cut ¼"-deep dadoes in the top (A) and bottom (B) to accept the sides (C). Then dado the sides to accept the center divider (D).

TOP. To complete the top first cut a slot to fit *your* miter gauge. (I used the miter gauge from my table saw.) Then,

rabbet the back edge to act as a sawdust relief; see Fig. la.

TOP OPENING. Finally, cut a 1"-wide notch on the back edge of the top (A) to provide an opening for sawdust and chips to fall through; see Fig. lb.

BACK PANEL. Now all that's left to make is the back panel (E). This panel provides a vertical surface to attach the router, and a fence for the workpiece to ride against.

To make the back panel, first cut a piece 10½" wide and 15¾" long out of ¾" plywood; see Fig. 2. Then cut a slot in the middle of the panel for the router bit. To do this, drill two 1"-dia. holes, 2" apart and then cut out the waste between the holes.

THREADED INSERTS. With the slot completed, the next step is to install four ¼" I.D. (inside diameter) threaded inserts in the back panel (E); see Fig. 2a. Two of these inserts are located on the front face for the guard adjustment knobs, and the other two are on the back face to allow the router to be adjusted up and down.

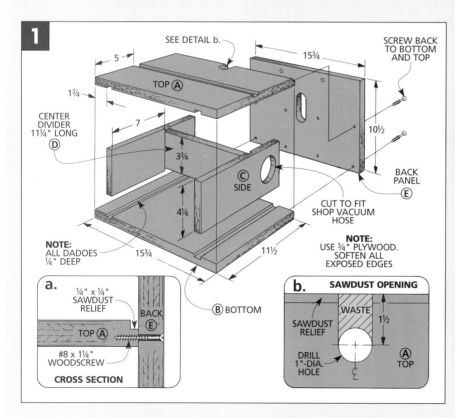

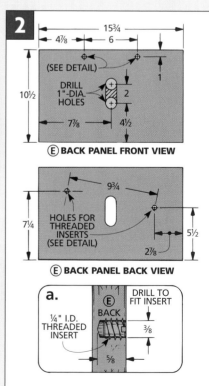

Note: It's important that the centers of the two holes on the back are exactly $9\frac{3}{4}$" apart. If they're not, the router plate won't fit.

ASSEMBLY. After the threaded inserts are installed, glue up all the pieces for the base frame. Then drill and countersink eight shank holes into the back panel (E) and screw it to the base; see Fig. 1.

ROUTER BASE PLATE

After completing the base frame, I made a new base plate for my router. This base plate provides a large surface to hold the router to the back panel (E).

CUT TO SIZE. To make the base plate (F), I started with a $\frac{1}{4}$"-thick piece of hardboard and cut it $7\frac{3}{4}$" wide and $11\frac{3}{4}$" long; see Fig. 3.

After the base plate is cut to size, drill a $1\frac{3}{4}$"-dia. hole in the center for the router bit to fit through. (Shop Note: The hole doesn't have to be perfectly round, so if you don't have a hole saw or a large drill bit you can cut it with a sabre saw.)

Next, drill and countersink holes in this plate so you can attach it to your router. To lay out the holes, remove the plastic base from your router and use it as a template.

MOUNTING HOLE. To mount the plate to the vertical back panel, first drill a $\frac{1}{4}$"-dia. mounting hole 3" down and 1" in from the right side of the base plate; see Fig. 3.

ADJUSTMENT SLOT. Now that the mounting hole is drilled, cut a $\frac{3}{8}$"-wide adjustment slot in the base plate; see Fig. 3. This slot provides a simple and accurate way to adjust the position of the router.

I cut this arched slot on a drill press by using the $\frac{1}{4}$" mounting hole as a pivot point; see Fig. 4. To do this, first drill a $\frac{1}{4}$"-dia. hole in a scrap piece of plywood and push a $\frac{1}{4}$" dowel in this hole. Then slip the mounting hole in the base plate (F) over the dowel.

Next, mount a $\frac{3}{8}$"-dia. drill bit and position the plywood so the distance from the center of the dowel to the center of the bit is $9\frac{3}{4}$". Then clamp the plywood to the drill press table.

Now drill a series of overlapping holes to create an arched slot; see Fig. 4. Then remove the base plate and clean out the slot with a file.

With the slot finished, I mounted the base plate (F) to the back panel with two plastic knobs and washers; see Fig. 5.

Note: You could use $\frac{3}{4}$"-long hex head bolts and washers instead of the plastic knobs.

GUARD

All that remains to complete the jig is a guard. Don't leave this guard off. It protects your fingers, and is needed to align your cuts; see Fig. 7.

UPRIGHTS. To make the guard, cut two uprights (G) from $\frac{1}{4}$"-thick hardboard, and then cut a $\frac{1}{2}$"-wide slot in each upright for the adjustment knobs; see Fig. 6. To attach the guard plate, glue a $\frac{1}{2}$"-thick block (H) to the bottom end of each upright.

GUARD PLATE. Next, I cut a guard plate (I) from $\frac{1}{4}$"-thick Plexiglas $1\frac{1}{2}$" wide and $7\frac{1}{2}$" long. (Note: If you can't find $\frac{1}{4}$"-thick Plexiglas, you can glue together two pieces of $\frac{1}{8}$"-thick Plexiglas.) Then I sanded a $\frac{1}{2}$" radius on the two outside corners and lightly sanded the front edges.

To mount the Plexiglas to the uprights, drill countersunk holes on the bottom side of the plate and screw the plate to the blocks; see Fig. 6a.

REFERENCE LINES. When the guard is screwed together, position it over the top of the bit. Then use an X-acto knife to scribe two lines on the bottom of the plate to align with each side of the bit; see Fig. 7. By using the lines as a guide, I know exactly where I'm starting and stopping a cut.

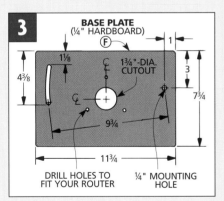

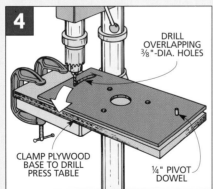

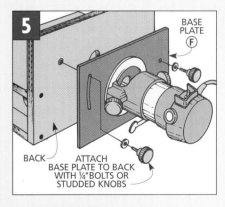

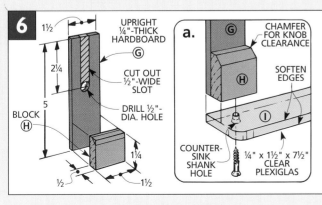

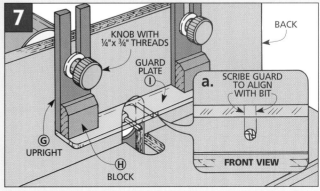

Mortise & Spline . . . . *Step-by-Step*

To make mortise and spline joints on the mortising table, start by adjusting the router so the bit is set to the correct height and depth; see Step 2.

Then adjust the guard to provide a reference for locating the ends of the mortise; see Step 3.

Now use a square to lay out the joint on both pieces; see Step 4. One advantage of this joint is that the mortises align automatically. Just mark the face side of both pieces and cut and assemble them with the marked sides facing *up*.

Finally, before you start cutting mortises be aware of the correct feed direction. Because the router is horizontal, the stock must be fed from left to right. This is the opposite of on a router table.

To cut end mortises, I use a miter gauge to support the workpiece; see Step 5. On edge mortises, I make a series of shallow cuts between the layout lines, pulling the piece away from the bit between each pass; see Step 7.

All that's left is to rip material for the splines ⅛" narrower than the length of the mortise; see Step 8. Then cut the splines to length ⅛" shorter than the combined depths of the mortises.

To glue up the joint, "butter" the inside of the mortises with a small artist's brush. Then, apply a thin film of glue to the spline and clamp; see Step 9.

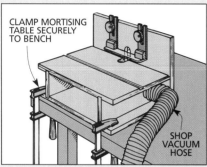

1 To have access to the front and left (feed) side of the mortising table clamp it to the left corner of the bench. Insert vacuum hose into hole in the side.

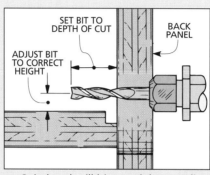

2 Spiral end mill bits work best. Adjust bit to produce the correct depth of cut. Then, adjust the router up or down until the bit is at the correct height.

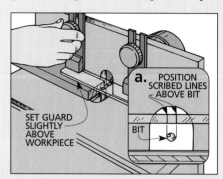

3 Tighten down the Plexiglas guard plate so it's slightly above the workpiece, and so the scribed lines in the plate are directly above the router bit.

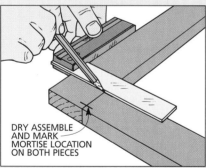

4 To mark the limits of both mortises, hold the pieces in their final position (at a right angle to each other), and draw lines across both faces.

5 Guide workpiece with miter gauge. (If end of workpiece is angled, angle miter gauge.) Then make two full-depth plunge cuts to define ends of mortise.

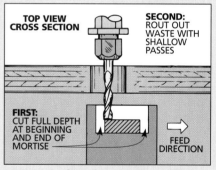

6 To complete the mortise, make several shallow cuts while moving the workpiece from left to right, and pulling the workpiece away between passes.

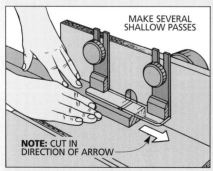

7 When cutting a mortise on the edge of a board, make shallow cuts, working from left to right. Use marks on guard to start and stop on the layout lines.

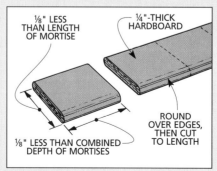

8 Cut spline material into strips ⅛" narrower than length of mortise. Round over edges. Cut splines to length ⅛" less than combined depth of mortises.

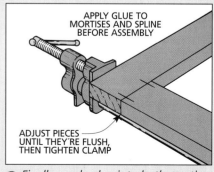

9 Finally, apply glue into both mortises and on the spline. Before clamping in place make sure the edges and faces of the adjoining pieces are flush.

Sources

One of the first things we take into consideration when designing projects at *Woodsmith* is whether the hardware is commonly available. Most of the hardware and supplies for the projects in this book can be found at local hardware stores or home centers. Sometimes, though, you may have to order it through the mail. In the box at right you'll find reputable national mail order sources and their phone numbers.

Also, *Woodsmith Project Supplies* offers hardware kits for some of the projects listed in this book (see box below).

Woodsmith Project Supplies

At the time of printing, the following project supply kits were available from *Woodsmith Project Supplies*. These kits include hardware (except as noted), but you must supply any lumber, plywood, or finish. For current prices and availability, call toll free:

1-800-444-7527

Scandinavian Corner Cabinet (pages 15-22) profile pattern only (no hardware kit) .... No. 8005–017

Country Pie Safe (pages 23-30) .... square nails, hardware, tin patterns, and tin

Country Hutch (pages 33-43) .... No. 796–100

Modular Cabinets (pages 45-52) .... knock-down fittings, Euro. hinges, shelf supports

Corner Cabinet (pages 56-65) .... No. 761–400

Display Cabinet (pages 66-73) .... No. 778–100

Gun Cabinet (pages 76-77) order Display Cabinet hardware (above), and then add locks .... No. 778–150 (each)

Armoire (pages 78-90) .... No. 767–300 raised panel bit......... No. 1514–391

Mortising Table (pages 92-93) .... No. 767–225 hardware & lumber ... No. 767–200

KEY: BX71

Mail Order Sources

Some of the most important "tools" we have in our shop are the mail order catalogs kept on the shelf. They're filled with special hardware, tools, finishes, lumber, and supplies that we can't always find at our local hardware store or home center.

I've found that these catalogs have excellent customer service and are only a phone call away. You should be able to find all the supplies for the projects in this book in one or more of these catalogs.

One more thing. It's amazing what you can learn about woodworking just by looking through these catalogs. If you don't have the following catalogs in your shop, I strongly recommend that you call and have each one sent to you. (And, of course, you'll be put on their never-ending mailing lists.)

Woodcraft
210 Wood Co. Industrial Park
P.O. Box 1686
Parkersburg, WV 26102-1686
800–225–1153
A must! Has just about everything (tools, hardware, finishing, wood) for the woodworker.

The Woodworkers' Store
4365 Willow Drive
Medina, MN 55340
800–279–4441
Probably the best all-around source for general and specialty hardware such as knock-down fittings and European hinges, but also has tools, finishes, lumber, and veneer.

Woodworker's Supply
1108 N. Glenn Road
Casper, WY 82601
800–645–9292
Excellent source for power tools and accessories, hardware, and finishes.

Trendlines
135 American Legion Highway
Revere, MA 02151
800–767–9999
Another complete source for power tools and accessories. Some hardware and supplies.

Tremont Nail Company
8 Elm Street
Wareham, MA 02571
800–842–0560
Over 175 years old and still making square nails and wrought iron hardware the old fashioned way. Great for projects like the pie safe.

WoodsmithShop Catalog
2200 Grand Avenue
Des Moines, IA 50312
800–444–7002
Our own source for practical jigs, useful tool accessories, *Woodsmith* project supplies, finishes, lumber, and kits.

Garrett Wade
161 Ave. of the Americas
New York, NY 10013
800–221–2942
The "Bible" for hand tools but also one of the best sources for finishing supplies and high quality power tools. This catalog is filled with useful information and tips for your shop. It reads more like a good woodworking book than a typical mail order catalog.

Constantines
2050 Eastchester Road
Bronx, NY 10461
800–223–8087
One of the original woodworking mail order catalogs. Known for veneers and inlays but also has a good collection of hardware and finishing supplies.

Country Accents
P.O. Box 437
Montoursville, PA 17754
717–478–4127
James and Marie Palotás have put together the most complete catalog of tin-punching supplies and designs you will find anywhere. Included are pre-punched tin, punching tools, and tin blanks.

If You Enjoyed This Book,
You're Going To Love Our Magazines

Woodworking and Home Improvement:

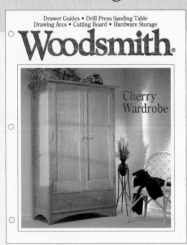

Drawer Guides • Drill Press Sanding Table
Drawing Arcs • Cutting Board • Hardware Storage

Woodsmith®

Cherry
Wardrobe

TIPS • TOOLS • TECHNIQUES

ShopNotes

Vol. 5   Issue 27

SLIDING
Cutoff Table

■ Scraper Plane ■ Outdoor Finishes ■ Picnic Table
■ Pegboard Storage Rack ■ Splined Miter Joinery

BENCH DESIGN CONTEST   CUSTOM MOLDING ■ DESK CLOCK ■ COPE & STICK JOINERY

WORKBENCH
THE ORIGINAL HOME WOODWORKING AND IMPROVEMENT MAGAZINE

Built-In
Bookcase

Chest of
Drawers

▲ *Woodsmith*, America's most popular fully-illustrated project magazine, continues to deliver detailed project plans, useful techniques, and easy-to-follow instructions to those who love woodworking. Published bi-monthly.

▲ *ShopNotes*, filled with practical tips and jigs, step-by-step woodworking techniques, shop projects and unbiased tool reviews, will help you get the most out of your shop, while saving you time and money! Published bi-monthly.

▲ *Workbench* contains creative furniture, shop, and woodworking home improvement projects, like kitchen cabinets, storage ideas, built-ins, decks, and more, all with detailed illustrations and photos. Published bi-monthly.

Gardening:

Gardening in Shade • **Tough Roses** • Container Gardening
The Right Mulch • Elegant Ornamental Grasses • **Trowels**

Garden Gate™
The Illustrated Guide to Home Gardening and Design

Great Annuals
to Mix With
Perennials

Cooking:

◀ Packed with practical, step-by-step gardening information, and hands-on tips and techniques about garden design and color, *Garden Gate* will help you create the beautiful garden you have always wanted. Published bi-monthly.

▶ Loaded with step-by-step photographs plus tips to help make your cooking easier and more eye-catching. *Cuisine* is the ideal bi-monthly magazine for those who love cooking and want to bring some variety to their dinner table.

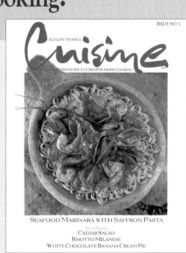

ISSUE NO 1

AUGUST HOME'S
Cuisine
ILLUSTRATED GUIDE TO CREATIVE HOME COOKING

SEAFOOD MARINARA WITH SAFFRON PASTA

also in this issue
CAESAR SALAD
RISOTTO MILANESE
WHITE CHOCOLATE BANANA CREAM PIE

To bring any of these exciting magazines to your home, or for more information,
Call Toll Free: 1-800-333-5075